Campaign

# Operation Barbarossa 1941 (2)

## Army Group North

MW00338322

OSPREY
PUBLISHING

# Operation Barbarossa 1941 (2)

## Army Group North

Robert Kirchubel · Illustrated by H Gerrard & P Dennis

Series editor Lee Johnson

First published in 2005 by Osprey Publishing
Midland House, West Way, Botley, Oxford OX2 0PH, UK
443 Park Avenue South, New York, NY 10016, USA
E-mail: info@ospreypublishing.com

© 2005 Osprey Publishing Ltd.

All rights reserved. Apart from any fair dealing for the purpose of private study,
research, criticism or review, as permitted under the Copyright, Designs and
Patents Act, 1988, no part of this publication may be reproduced, stored in a
retrieval system, or transmitted in any form or by any means, electronic,
electrical, chemical, mechanical, optical, photocopying, recording or otherwise,
without the prior written permission of the copyright owner. Inquiries should be
addressed to the Publishers.

A CIP catalog record for this book is available from the British Library.

ISBN 1 84176 857 X

Editor: Lee Johnson
Design: The Black Spot
Index by Alan Thatcher
Maps by The Map Studio
3D bird's-eye views by The Black Spot
Battlescene artwork by Peter Dennis and Howard Gerrard
Originated by The Electronic Page Company, Cwmbran, UK
Printed in China through World Print Ltd.

05 06 07 08 09   10 9 8 7 6 5 4 3 2 1

For a catalog of all books published by Osprey please contact:

NORTH AMERICA
Osprey Direct, 2427 Bond Street, University Park, IL 60466, USA
E-mail: info@ospreydirectusa.com

ALL OTHER REGIONS
Osprey Direct UK, P.O. Box 140, Wellingborough, Northants, NN8 2FA, UK
E-mail: info@ospreydirect.co.uk

www.ospreypublishing.com

## Author's note

This book is written to the glory of God. The author wishes
to thank the following for their contributions to its success:
my wife Linda and sons Erich, Mason, and Marc for their
forbearance; friends Gary Komar, Mal Russell, and Joe
Wilson for their editorial assistance; the ladies of the
Inter-Library Loan Department of the San Joaquin County
Library for helping bring the death and destruction of the
Ostfront to small-town California; Greg Vose for information
on the Baltic States today; Pauli Kruhse for information on
the Finnish Army; and, my superiors at the California
National Guard for their assistance.

The author made every reasonable effort to contact the
copyright holders for the photographs used in this book but
in some cases could not trace them.

## Artists' note

Readers may care to note that the original paintings from
which the color plates in this book were prepared are
available for private sale. All reproduction copyright
whatsoever is retained by the Publishers. All inquiries
should be addressed to:

Howard Gerrard
11 Oaks Road
Tenterden
Kent
TN30 6RD
UK

Peter Dennis
Fieldhead
The Park
Mansfield
Nottinghamshire
NG18 2AT
UK

The Publishers regret that they can enter into no
correspondence upon this matter.

## KEY TO MILITARY SYMBOLS

# CONTENTS

# INTRODUCTION

Nazi Germany's invasion of the Soviet Union on 22 June 1941, Operation Barbarossa, has no equal in military history. By nearly any measure – numbers of combatants, physical scope, hatred, and ruination – the Nazi–Soviet war was immense. Germany's Führer Adolf Hitler achieved strategic, operational, and tactical surprise against an amply forewarned Josef Stalin. Rapacious panzer groups, supported overhead by the Luftwaffe, recorded daily advances of 30 and 40 miles. The bulk of the Wehrmacht marched on foot behind, closing off pockets of many hundreds of thousands of Red Army captives. Nazi Propaganda Minister Josef Goebbels demurred at showing the German people maps of the USSR, worried that they would be unnerved by the immense distances involved, while some Germans wondered if, prior to launching Barbarossa, Hitler had even seen such a map.

While the Soviet Union's mass was obvious to anyone looking at a globe of the earth, the inner strength of the Communist government, the toughness of the Red Army soldier, and the ultimate wisdom of its leadership's conduct of the war came as an unexpected shock to the invaders and many observers. The German Armed Forces' initial low opinion of the Red Army was not unreasonable given its recent dismal performance in battle with the Finns during the Winter War of 1939–40. From the very start the vicious border battles demonstrated to the Wehrmacht in the field, if not to its leaders behind, that the Barbarossa campaign would not be another walkover. Many Soviet soldiers were cut off behind enemy lines in huge encirclements, but far from surrendering they either fought to the death or slipped away into Russia's vast swamps and forests to join the partisans. By the time the first freezing weather hit in October, the Wehrmacht was greatly weakened and still far from achieving most of its objectives.

Both Hitler and his professional military staffs were practically unanimous in their rosy expectations of the invasion's results. Barbarossa's ultimate outcome was far from clear at any point during the summer of 1941. The Wehrmacht's "Blitzkrieg" (lightning war) – the combination of flexible mission-style orders, mechanization, airpower, and communications – won victory after victory. Having vanquished the French, the world's "best army," the year before, Germany had a confidence in her armed forces that bordered on arrogance. The Soviet military did not obligingly collapse, however, nor did an alternative to the Communist system present itself. First Hitler, then Stalin, called for a total war of extermination and national survival. Interestingly, only in the minds of the two dictators did the political and military strategy of either country coalesce. The war on the Eastern Front, and it might be argued Barbarossa itself, sealed the fate of Hitler's Third Reich and determined the outcome of World War II.

OPPOSITE **Too gentlemanly for the Nazi–Soviet war and too conservative for the Blitzkrieg? Von Leeb probably possessed the wrong temperament for the Germans to succeed. (US National Archives)**

The battlefields portrayed here long possessed military significance for the Germans and the peoples of eastern Europe. Here the Teutonic Knights sought to Christianize the heathen via the edge of the sword, the Prussians under David von Yorck abandoned Napoleon to join Tsar Alexander and the *Freikorps* battled Bolsheviks after World War I. Finland represented a prize historically coveted by both Sweden and Russia.

Army Group North's Field Marshal Wilhelm *Ritter* von Leeb had not been tested in either the German conquest of Poland in 1939 or in the assault on France and the Low Countries. He had neither led panzer formations nor worked with his commanders prior to *Barbarossatag*, 22 June 1941. While Army Group North's operational area might be the smallest of those assigned to the three German army groups, so were its forces. The terrain between East Prussia and Leningrad was some of the worst encountered by the *Ostheer*, and possessed a transportation infrastructure that was at best primitive. Army Group North's primary objective, Leningrad – a city of 3,000,000 souls – had ideological and economic significance for both sides. However, at no time did Hitler provide von Leeb with the resources necessary to conquer it.

In the extreme north, German *Gebirgsjäger* (mountain troops) battled futilely toward Murmansk across frozen tundra. Both climate and terrain in this region were alien to the Germans, earning them the thinly disguised contempt of their Finnish allies and Soviet enemies alike. Disjointed Axis command and control created numerous liabilities; von Leeb's main front fell under the *Oberkommando des Heeres* (OKH), Finnish Marshal Carl Mannerheim commanded his country's effort northwest of Leningrad, while the *Oberkommando der Wehrmacht* (OKW) controlled Axis operations near the Arctic Circle. To compound German problems, Finland's military ambitions did not extend beyond regaining territory lost to the Soviet Union in 1939–40; Mannerheim proved unwilling to cross much beyond the 1939 boundary in order to link up with von Leeb.

An SdKfz 10 prime mover half-track towing a 37mm PAK through a burning village. The death and destruction of Barbarossa rivaled that of the Thirty Years War. (History in the Making)

German logistics, intended for a brief Blitzkrieg, naturally failed in a sustained war of attrition.

Soviet arrangements were not markedly better. At the highest level, the Northwest Front suffered from weak leadership; its commander, Lieutenant General F.I. Kuznetsov proved completely incapable. His successor, Marshal K.E. Voroshilov demonstrated heroic leadership, but poor managerial skills. As with all Red Army forces on 22 June, the Northwest Front defended exposed, ill-prepared positions; the relative security of the Stalin Line defenses had been left behind during the Soviet land-grab of 1939–40.

The Northern Front under Lieutenant General M.M. Popov, guarding Leningrad and the Finnish border, gave a better account of itself. Popov exploited Finland's limited war aims around Leningrad and allowed a skillful subordinate, Lieutenant General V.A. Frolov, to frustrate the Axis in the far north.

After the shock of the campaign's first few days wore off, Luftwaffe elements enforced their will on the Soviets only with substantial reinforcement, and the size of the Finnish area of operations dissipated the small Luftwaffe effort there. Throughout Barbarossa German soldiers repeatedly shot at their Luftwaffe comrades because they saw German aircraft so seldom that they assumed any aircraft to be Soviet. On the other hand, the Red Air Force soon recovered to represent a persistent threat to the invaders. At sea the large and prestigious Red Banner Baltic Fleet remained passive against the relatively small Kriegsmarine elements in the Baltic Sea. However, Soviet Northern Fleet elements constantly harassed the Germans in the Arctic Ocean and its littoral.

# THE CAMPAIGN'S ORIGINS

### Germany

S.J. Lewis described Barbarossa as "the only war Hitler ever wanted." The Führer saw Bolshevism as the most extreme form of "international Jewry" and set forth plans for a new order as early as his writings in *Mein Kampf* and even more in his second book of 1928. Just days after taking power, on 3 February 1933, he told skeptical *Reichswehr* leaders of his desire to conquer *Lebensraum* (space to live) in the east.

After years of antagonism, on 28 August 1939, Nazi Germany and the Soviet Union shocked most of the world by signing a nonaggression pact. Hitler said the pact was "misunderstood by many [Nazi] party members" and had to reassure Italian dictator Benito Mussolini the agreement was only a temporary move. The Führer put his freedom to good use, crushing all opposition in continental non-Russian Europe – all with the Soviet leader's tacit approval.

Hitler had little energy for the Battle of Britain or the complex invasion of Great Britain. OKW Operations Chief, General of Artillery Alfred Jodl, admitted that English "stoic equanimity" would carry them through the bombing and that there was no indication that the air war would cause their collapse. Germany was even less capable of bringing her military forces to bear on the United States. As bizarre as this may sound to the modern reader, the Führer settled on attacking the Soviet Union as the best way to defeat the Anglo-American maritime powers.

Red Army riflemen advance with the support of a Maxim M1910 machine gun (left) and 50mm M1940/1941 mortar (right). The defense of the USSR ultimately depended on men like these. (History in the Making)

Therefore, even before beginning the Battle of Britain, Hitler instructed the Wehrmacht to plan an invasion of the USSR. With the Red Army emasculated and with Russia's resources at her disposal, the Reich would be America's equal. Almost to a man Germany's military leadership counseled Hitler against attacking. Luftwaffe leader Hermann Göring's opposition must have been the harshest blow: Hitler told the Reichsmarschall, "Why don't you stop trying to persuade me to drop my plans for Russia. I've made up my mind."

Any pretense of long-term Nazi–Soviet cooperation vanished with Soviet Foreign Minister V.M. Molotov's visit to Berlin on 12–13 November 1940. It was an open secret in the capital that Hitler expected to score a diplomatic coup; he would offer Stalin a free hand against the British possessions in south-west Asia in exchange for German dominance of Central and Eastern Europe and the Mediterranean. But Molotov had no intention of accepting Hitler's plans and came to Berlin with his own agenda, even resurrecting Soviet interests in Finland. Hitler believed continuing British resistance had emboldened the USSR and, enraged by this rebuff, formalized the plans for Operation Barbarossa within a month.

### Finland

As part of the restructuring of Europe's power structure in 1809 by the French Emperor Napoleon Bonaparte, Finland became a Russian grand duchy and for the next 100 years the Finns strained under the Russian yoke. During the Russian Civil War, with the help of a German corps, White (as opposed to "Red" Bolshevik) forces under Mannerheim won Finnish independence. In the Winter War of 1939–40 the Soviet Union took her revenge. Stalin launched the Red Army against Finland and, despite an inept performance from the Soviets and heroic resistance by the Finns, the result was inevitable. Finland lost 23,000 killed, 45,000 wounded, and had to evacuate 420,000 people from lands ceded to the Soviets. While Stalin secured Leningrad he created a dangerous enemy.

In August 1940, the USSR once more massed troops on the Finnish border, making new demands on Finland. Three months later came the first tentative contacts between German and Finnish military planners. Führer Directive 21 allowed Finland a modest role in Barbarossa while relations between the two countries warmed. Hitler wanted Finnish assistance in three main areas: pressure on Leningrad, help against the Arctic ports and the Murmansk railroad, and raw materials – especially the nickel mines at Petsamo. Eager to avenge losses suffered during the Winter War, Finland agreed to most of the German expectations. However, Finland was not at war and Helsinki crawled with foreign diplomats. Partly as a result, Hitler kept Finland out of serious planning until late May 1941. Finland's limited goals for World War II were: freedom from Soviet intimidation, reliable sources of food, and restoration of the 1939 borders.

### Soviet Union

In 1939 Stalin's primary concern remained establishing "socialism in one country." He strengthened the USSR by expanding the military and by ruthlessly and brutally developing Soviet industry with successive Five Year Plans; the USSR was in the midst of the Third Plan in 1941. He created an entirely new resource and industrial base beyond the range of any potential enemy. Output of numerous strategic materials was only slightly higher than Germany's, but the Soviet growth rate was much greater.

In the summer of 1939 Stalin went along with Hitler's nonaggression pact. Britain and France had sacrificed Czechoslovakia the year before to buy a few months' peace; the USSR sacrificed Poland. The Soviet leader's opinion of the pact was little different from Hitler's, indeed Stalin admitted at the Yalta Conference that the pact was "not serious." While one of Hitler's intentions was that the pact should spread distrust

A camouflaged bunker on the original Stalin Line west of Pskov captured in mid-July. Much of the line's weaponry had been stripped a year earlier as the Red Army redeployed west after the seizure of eastern Poland, Bessarabia and the Baltic States, rendering many of the defenses of doubtful value. (US National Archives)

and chaos among his enemies, Stalin sought stability to carry through his vast restructuring of the Soviet Union. Ruthlessly consolidating power, Stalin purged some 15,000–30,000 officers from his military during the 1930s, and these mostly from the highest ranks. Over 8,000,000 Soviet citizens were in jail at any one time from 1937–53, and of those 1,000,000 died each year. Stalin took his final step to power on 5 May 1941 when he added the title of Soviet Premier to that of Communist Party Chairman.

Red Army failings during the 1939–40 Winter War were legion and only by applying overwhelming violence and numbers did the USSR finally prevail. While Hitler's war machine swept all before it, Soviet weaknesses were an embarrassment. In accordance with the secret protocols of the Nazi–Soviet nonaggression pact, Stalin occupied the Baltic States and Rumanian Bessarabia as part of the "Expansion of the Fraternal Family of Soviet Nations." With these moves, and the occupation of eastern Poland the year before, the Red Army's frontlines were shorter, requiring fewer units to garrison them. The Soviets largely squandered the advantages of this buffer zone by abandoning its fortifications 200–400 miles behind, and through their imprudent forward deployment. This surge westward demonstrates the Stalinist military dilettantism that plagued Soviet operations well into Barbarossa.

# CHRONOLOGY

**November 1939–March 1940** Russo-Finnish Winter War

## 1940

**5 August** General Marcks completes his *Operationsentwurf Ost*.
**7 August** OKW completes *Aufbau Ost*.
**12–13 November** Molotov visits Berlin.
**18 November** Soviets learn German invasion includes attack on Leningrad.
**28 November–3 December** Paulus hosts Barbarossa wargames.
**5 December** Hitler approves basic plan.
**17–20 December** Barbarossa logistical wargames.
**18 December** Führer Directive 21 issued.
**23 December–13 January, 1941** Kremlin command conferences and wargames; another shake-up within Soviet high command.

## 1941

**31 January** *Aufmarschanweisung Ost* published.
**25–27 May** Finnish Chief of Staff visits OKW.
**12 June** Kriegsmarine begins mining Baltic.
**22 June** *Barbarossatag*. German invasion begins. Soviet Military Districts become fronts.
**24–29 June** Battle of Raseiniai, XLI Panzer Corps against 12th Mechanized Corps.
**26 June** LVI Panzer Corps captures Dünaburg bridgehead.
**29 June–6 July** Mountain Corps Norway's first attack across Litsa River.
**30 June** Sobennikov replaces Kuznetsov as commander of the Northwest Front.
**1 July** XXXVI Corps and Finns attack at Salla.
**9 July** Piadyshev takes command of LOG.
**10 July** Voroshilov arrives at Northwest Direction; Finns attack in Karelia north of Lake Ladoga.
**13–17 July** Mountain Corps Norway's second attack across Litsa River.
**14 July** 6th Panzer Division achieves bridgehead over the River Narva.
**14–18 July** 11th Army counterattack against LVI Panzer Corps at Soltsy.
**19 July** Führer Directive 33 issued.
**21 July** Hitler visits Army Group North headquarters.
**23 July** Supplement to Führer Directive issued.
**30 July** Führer Directive 34 published.
**31 July** Finns attack in Karelia south of Lake Ladoga.
**8–10 August** German general offensive on Luga River begins.
**12 August** Supplement to Führer Directive 34 issued; 11th, 27th, 34th, 48th Armies attack Sixteenth Army at Staraya Russa.

**19 August** LVI Panzer Corps counterattacks to Staraya Russa.
**22 August** Hitler issues *Denkschrift* ending high command debate.
**26 August** LVII Panzer from Army Group Center captures Velikie Luki.
**28 August** Tallinn falls to XLII Corps.
**29 August** Vyborg taken by Finnish IV Corps.
**1 September** XXXVI Corps and Finns unite at Allakurtti.
**2 September** Von Brauchitsch and Halder visit Army Group North headquarters.
**8 September** Finns reach Svir River; XXXIX Panzer Corps captures Shlisselburg encircling Leningrad.
**8–20 September** Mountain Corps Norway's third attack across Litsa River.
**9 September** Zhukov arrives in Leningrad; XLI Panzer Corps renews assault toward Krasnogvardeysk.
**14 September** Amphibious assault on Muhu Island.
**15 September** Germans assault Saaremaa Island.
**16 September** XLI Panzer Corps occupies Strelnya, 8th Army cut off from Leningrad.
**22 September** Germans issue directive on starvation of Leningrad.
**25 September** Frontlines around Leningrad essentially solidify for duration of siege.
**1 October** Finnish VII Corps takes Petrozavodsk.
**12 October** Attack of Hiiumaa Island.
**16 October** XXXIX Panzer Corps begins attack toward Tikhvin.
**26 October** Von Leeb visits the Führer's Headquarters.
**8 November** Tikhvin falls.
**12 November** 52nd Army counterattack at Volkhov.
**15 November** Finnish Group "F" links up on Kandalaksha axis.
**19 November** 4th Army launches attack to recapture Tikhvin.
**6 December** Finnish II Corps and Group "O" take Medvezh'yegorsk.
**7 December** Germans evacuate Tikhvin.
**Mid-December** Frontlines stabilize on Volkhov River.

## 1942

**16 January** Hitler relieves von Leeb as Army Group North Commander.

# OPPOSING PLANS

## GERMAN PLANS

German planning for Barbarossa began within weeks of the French surrender. Oberquartiermeister Lieutenant General Friedrich Paulus wrote after the war that "experts declared [Hitler's] previous victories impossible;" the Wehrmacht would again prove them wrong in 1941. While many of Hitler's generals questioned Barbarossa as an indirect attack on Britain, they were enthusiastic about building a blockade-proof Reich.

On 4 July 1940 Army Chief of Staff Colonel General Franz Halder put Generals Georg Kuechler and Erich Marcks to work planning the Eighteenth Army's defense of the east. Their planning turned offensive two weeks later when Hitler told Halder, "Stalin kokettiert mit England" ("Stalin flirts with England"). Lieutenant Colonel Eberhardt Kinzel, head of Army intelligence at *Fremde Heere Ost* (Foreign Armies East – FHO), created in four days the poor analysis of the Red Army that the Wehrmacht would take to its grave. This junior officer and his over-worked staff also had responsibility for the armies of Scandinavia, the Balkans, China, Japan, and the United States. The Gestapo, answerable for political intelligence, added inaccuracies by predicting the Soviet state's collapse in weeks.

By the end of July, Marcks' planning was nearing completion. Following Kinzel he assumed "… the Russians no longer possess the superiority of numbers they had in the World War …" On 29 July he flew to Halder's

**Red Army soldier crawls to surrender to a Panzer IV and attendant *Landsers*. The barn is well built and undamaged, a valuable refuge in the coming winter. (History in the Making)**

headquarters in Fontainebleau where the Army Chief of Staff succeeded in shifting Marcks' emphasis from the Ukraine to Moscow. Marcks completed his *Operationsentwurf Ost* (Operational Draft East) on 5 August 1940. In general he discussed two main groupings, north and south of the Rokitno Marshes. Regarding Army Group North, he wrote "north of the main group of forces [aiming for Moscow] a strong group advances through the Baltic states to Leningrad and takes the base of the Russian Fleet." He anticipated the advance on the axis Dünaburg–Pskov–Leningrad.

Hitler wanted OKW involved so on 29 July he told Jodl to also prepare a plan. The resulting estimate by Lieutenant Colonel Bernhard von Lossberg is known as *Aufbau Ost* (Buildup East). He completed an additional *Operationsstudie Ost* (Operational Study East) on 15 September 1940. Von Lossberg likewise envisioned the *Schwerpunkt* (focal point) against Stalin's capital, planned to annihilate the Red Army west of the Dvina River, and called for German troops in Norway and the Finns to cut the Murmansk railroad and to cooperate with forces advancing from East Prussia to encircle Leningrad.

A horse-drawn supply column passes an old castle on the banks of the Narva River. Army Group North halted numerous times during Barbarossa to allow supplies to catch up with the leading units. (US National Archives)

General Paulus gathered these studies and began formal planning in September. Paulus approached the problem "from the purely military point of view." He supervised wargames in late November and early December. These centered on the Baltic states and Leningrad, and less on Moscow. Prophetically, the wargames indicated that clearing the Baltic states would take much time and impact Army Group Center operations.

On 5 December von Brauchitsch and Halder briefed Hitler with the results. The Führer stressed "We must strive to encircle the enemy forces in the Baltics. Therefore the Moscow Army Group must be so strong that it can turn significant portions to the north." Ironically Hitler dashed Army Group North's chances of success when he failed to heed his own advice.

Von Lossberg wrote the first draft of Führer Directive 21 on 12 December, the Luftwaffe added its details on the 16th, it went to Hitler the next day and became official on the 18th. A series of logistical wargames were held from 17 to 20 December, *after* Hitler signed the Directive! The Wehrmacht believed its logistics nearly failed in France because the theater was so large (*sic!*) and required serious reworking for Barbarossa. These wargames confirmed the requirement for a logistics pause at the Dvina–Dnepr rivers. Finally, they proved that if the Soviet military was not destroyed west of that line, the abysmal infrastructure further east meant the Germans probably would not succeed against even weak resistance.

OKH published its operation order, *Aufmarschanweisung Ost* (Deployment Directive East), on 31 January 1941. It confirmed the primacy of encircling the Red Army west of the Dvina, leading with a strong right and the *Schwerpunkt* along the axis Dünaburg––Opochka–Leningrad. Field Marshal von Leeb's main goals were: destroy the Red Army holding the Baltic states, neutralize Kronshtadt, capture Leningrad, and link up with the Finns.

Army Group North's plan for reaching Leningrad, 500 miles away, went as follows: Hoepner's Panzer Group would punch through the Soviet's frontier defenses and make for the Dvina crossings near Dünaburg, from there aiming toward Opochka. Depending on Leningrad's defenses, Hoepner would either advance due north or swing northeast. The Eighteenth Army would clear the Baltic region and be prepared to take the islands off Estonia's coast. The Sixteenth Army had responsibility for securing the boundary with Army Group Center.

General Paulus' wargames demonstrated that if Eighteenth Army was strengthened at the expense of the Sixteenth, the Army Group Center flank would be vulnerable to Soviet counterattacks. Threats to their common boundary did indeed cause constant friction between the two army groups. The wargames also established the need for intermediate objectives near Velikie Luki or Lake Il'men preparatory to an assault on Leningrad. Propitiously they confirmed a requirement for the loan of some Army Group Center Panzers if von Leeb hoped to conquer the city.

Some historians falsely believe Germany's Balkan invasion fatally delayed the launching of Operation Barbarossa. Von Lossberg wrote that Hitler always planned to conquer Greece prior to Barbarossa. Invading the Balkans was discussed at the Führer conference of 5 December. The main causes for deferring Barbarossa's start date from 15 May to 22 June were incomplete logistical arrangements, and an unusually wet winter that kept rivers at full flood until late spring. Ironically, Army Group North felt the impact of the Balkan operation worst; when Hitler dispatched the Twelfth Army against Yugoslavia and Greece he moved the Eleventh from OKH Reserve and sent it south. Only five of 21 divisions (none mechanized) from the Eleventh ever appeared on von Leeb's order of battle, despite his desperate need for them.

Differences between Hitler and his generals, and between OKH and OKW were discounted by the German high command's expectation that their Russian campaign would be short. With near-unanimity they assumed Barbarossa would begin with the quick elimination of the Red Army followed by a series of marches and a brutal occupation. The planned final assault on Moscow was predicated on the two northern army groups cooperating to capture Leningrad and Kronshtadt before wheeling southeast. However, the planned one-two punch never occurred.

# SOVIET PLANS

Marshal M.N. Tukhachevsky was the bright star of the Red Army in the early 1930s. His execution in May 1937, accused amongst other crimes of sabotage, began the avalanche of murder known as the Great Purges. One reason Stalin considered the marshal a saboteur was the weak state of the defenses on the approaches to Leningrad.

Thanks to its extensive and effective spy network the USSR learned of Barbarossa soon after Wehrmacht leaders. Initially, the Soviets planned to defend critical axes of advance using their fortified regions. That plan ceased to be workable when the Soviet Union extended its borders west in 1939–40. The decision to deploy defending units so far forward also robbed the Red Army of room to maneuver – a traditional Russian strength.

As Red Army Chief of Staff and member of the Military Soviet from 1926–34, Tukhachevsky focused on defending the Ukraine and the twin "capitals" of Moscow and Leningrad. By 1940, however, much had changed and the German Blitzkrieg campaigns had turned the military world on its head. While Stalin acted the good neighbor to assuage

Hitler, Soviet military thinkers put Tukhachevsky's offensive doctrines on hold until they had found a way to halt the Blitzkrieg.

The Red Army began planning in earnest immediately following Hitler's "secret" 31 July 1940 meeting. Following Stalin's contributions, Mobilization Plan 41 (MP 41) was published in October 1940. Results of wargames in December and January of 1941 painted a gloomy picture. On 13 January Stalin asked "Who won here?" None of his generals answered satisfactorily. Stalin made General G.K. Zhukov Red Army Chief of Staff two weeks later.

Even the USSR's best general could not work defensive miracles in less than five months. His State Defensive Plan 41 (DP 41) stated "that the Red Army would begin military operations in response to an aggressive attack." While remaining on the strategic defensive it would unleash operational offensives that might penetrate into the Reich; the Soviets were also aware of the panzer thrusts' lack of mutual support and vulnerable flanks.

Fatefully, Zhukov's plans also called for the forward deployment of 237 out of 303 divisions. The opening of the Barbarossa offensive on 22 June came too soon for MP 41 and DP 41 to take effect. On that date the Red Army was deployed as follows: First Echelon (6–30 miles deep) – 57 divisions, Second Echelon (30–60 miles) – 52 divisions, Third Echelon (60–240 miles) – 62 divisions. This positioning of so much of the Red Army in forward areas played into the Germans' hands.

Initial planning in the north assumed that Leningrad would only be threatened from Finland and that German thrusts would aim for Moscow. By 18 November 1940 the Soviets learned of the existence in German planning of a supporting attack heading for Leningrad. A defensive plan from that date identified an attack axis through Pskov and anticipated the Finns advancing via Vyborg against Leningrad. Responsibility for defending the Pskov–Ostrov approaches to Bolshevism's birthplace shifted to the Baltic Special Military District from the Leningrad Military District. Unfortunately for the Soviets, neither headquarters gave the issue its full attention.

Such plans as did exist identified two phases of defensive fighting: first at the frontier and along the Dvina River, second on the line Riga–Pskov–Luga–Novgorod. This took advantage of natural obstacles like the Velikaya and Luga Rivers, as well as marshes and forests in the area. A later plan, dated 15 May 1941, maintained Leningrad Military District responsibility for defending Leningrad and the Murmansk rail line. The same plan gave the Baltic Special Military District the mission to halt the enemy between Riga and Vilnius and hold the Baltic Islands. The "Leningraders" would accomplish their assigned mission. Their comrades on the East Prussian border would not.

The "1941 Plan for the Defense of State Borders" assumed Germany would need 10–15 days to finalize their invasion. However, Stalin preferred to look the other way as the Wehrmacht prepared for 11 months. One observer called Hitler the only man Stalin ever trusted. The dictator's wishful thinking was not the Soviets' sole intelligence weakness. They over-estimated German strength at 260 divisions, 10,000 tanks and 15,000 aircraft (real numbers: 150, 3,300, and 2,510 respectively). However, 500,000 untrained recruits and reserve armies sent to the front in the weeks prior to *Barbarossatag* could not stave off disaster.

**Kuznetsov barely lasted a fortnight before being relieved of command. The Soviets' prewar assumption was that the Germans would largely bypass Kuznetsov's Northwest Front as they drove for Moscow; thus, he was ill-prepared for Army Group North's onslaught. (David Glantz)**

# OPPOSING COMMANDERS

Generals Hoepner, seen here on a field telephone, and von Reinhardt led the main panzer drive toward Leningrad. Von Reinhardt's XI Panzer Corps bore the brunt of the fighting for the city while von Manstein struggled on a more easterly bearing. (Scharnhorst Verlag)

## AXIS COMMANDERS

**Field Marshal Wilhelm *Ritter* von Leeb** commanded Army Group North. A Bavarian artillery officer, he served in China in the Boxer Rebellion. During the Great War he earned the Bavarian Max Josef Order and non-hereditary title of *Ritter*. During the interwar years he authored *Defense*, which even the German editor of his diary called "essentially unnoticed then and forgotten today."

Von Leeb was a devout Catholic and anti-Nazi. He asked to be relieved of his command on 16 January 1942 and Hitler never recalled him. The Nuremberg tribunal sentenced von Leeb to three years in prison and he died in 1956.

**Colonel General Georg von Küchler**, another career artillery officer, commanded the Eighteenth Army. During the campaign in the West the Eighteenth captured Dunkirk. Von Küchler succeeded von Leeb but his command of Army Group North was uninspired. After the war he served six years in prison and died in 1969.

Sixteenth Army Commander **Colonel General Ernst Busch** is considered a pro-Nazi. After commanding VIII Corps in Poland and the Sixteenth Army for four years, he took over Army Group Center, presiding over that organization's destruction in the summer of 1944. He died of a heart attack in British captivity in July 1945 and was buried in an unmarked grave.

A lifelong cavalry officer, **Colonel General Erich Hoepner** commanded von Leeb's mobile formation, Panzer Group Four. In 1938 anti-Hitler army leaders earmarked his 1st Light Division to hold off SS units in Munich if the Czech crisis went badly for Germany. Hoepner commanded the XVI Panzer Corps in Poland and France. Following Barbarossa, his renamed Fourth Panzer Army transferred to Army Group Center and bore the brunt of the fighting for Moscow.

Hoepner has an anti-Nazi reputation but nevertheless on 2 May 1941 wrote the obligatory letter describing the upcoming "Battle for the existence of the German *Volk*" against "Jewish Bolshevism." In January 1942 he disobeyed Hitler's "No Retreat" order. The Führer accused him of "disobedience before the enemy," "endangering my authority as Supreme Commander" and ordered Hoepner "cashiered with all the resulting consequences." Implicated in the conspiracy surrounding the July 1944 attempt to assassinate Hitler, SS men hanged him that August.

**Colonel General Nikolas von Falkenhorst** commanded German forces operating from Norway and Central Finland. In 1918 he served in Finland as part of the German forces sent there to ensure the country's independence. In 1940, von Falkenhorst led the joint conquest of

Axis commanders in Finland von Falkenhorst and Mannerheim. The Finnish border with the USSR was two thirds as long as the main front from Memel to the Black Sea. However, the theater was doomed as a strategic backwater plagued by complicated command relationships and few mutual objectives. (Ediciones Dolmen)

Scandinavia. The Nuremberg tribunal condemned him to death but commuted the sentence.

Two corps commanders are especially noteworthy: **General of Infantry Erich von Manstein**, commander of LVI Panzer Corps, had a superlative reputation well before Barbarossa and went on to become one of the most highly regarded German generals of World War II.

Bavarian **General of Mountain Troops Eduard Dietl** joined the pre-Nazi German Workers' Party in 1919, before Hitler. The "Hero of Narvik" died in an air crash in June 1944.

Among the Luftwaffe generals supporting Army Group North, *Luftflotte 1* commander, **Colonel General Alfred Keller** was an "old eagle" (pre-1914 aviator). He joined the new Luftwaffe in 1935, rose through various high commands only to retire in 1943. **Lieutenant General Helmuth Förster**, also a decorated World War I aviator, took command of *I Fliegerkorps* when the Royal Air Force shot down his predecessor shortly before Barbarossa. He left operational command for an Air Ministry staff position in 1942. *Luftflotte 5* commander, **Colonel General Jürgen Stumpff** was a World War I staff officer who became Chief of the Luftwaffe General Staff during the interwar years. He commanded in the far north, attacking Arctic convoys such as PQ17 until November 1943, when he was reassigned to command the Reich's air defense. Stumpff represented the Luftwaffe at the 8 May 1945 surrender ceremony.

A large number of these commanders earned the *Pour le Merite*: Busch, Keller, Siegfried Haenicke (61st Infantry Division), Otto Lancelle (121st Infantry Division), and Ferdinand Schörner (6th Mountain Division). Lieutenant General Franz von Roques commanded von Leeb's rear security forces, the same position held by his younger brother Karl in Army Group South.

Finnish **Marshal Carl Gustav Mannerheim** was descended from that nation's earlier Swedish nobility. A Tsarist Guards Cavalry officer, he was commended for bravery at Port Arthur and Mukden. He served in cavalry divisions and corps on the Austro-Hungarian and Rumanian

Frolov was one of the few Red Army leaders to survive Barbarossa. His command of Soviet forces in the far north benefited from a number of factors: unity of command, superior logistics, relatively large naval contingent, and good lateral rail lines. (David Glantz)

fronts in World War I, before returning to his homeland where he won further acclaim during the Finnish War of Independence in 1918. He resigned in 1919 but returned to service in 1933 and fought a brilliant defensive campaign against the Red Army during the Winter War of 1939–40. He signed but withdrew numerous letters of resignation during World War II. The Finnish people elected him president in 1944 and he died in 1951.

## SOVIET COMMANDERS

**Lieutenant General F.I. Kuznetsov** commanded the Northwest Front. He was one of Stalin's most senior generals and although a well-regarded theoretician, had no combat experience on *Barbarossatag*. The official Soviet history of the war noted that Kuznetsov suffered from liabilities common to most other Front commanders: he was "unprepared to cope with the exceptionally complicated task" and "lacked the necessary operational and strategic preparation and practice." He commanded the Front only until 30 June. He later commanded the Central Front in July, until the Germans destroyed it a month later, and led the ill-fated 51st Army defending the Crimea in September. After he failed in that mission, Stalin shifted him to command of the 61st Army until he lost that job because of his alcoholism.

**Marshal K.E. Voroshilov** replaced Kuznetsov as commander of the Northwest Front. He had joined the Communist Party in 1903 and was active in the October Revolution and Russian Civil War. During the latter he served in the 1st Cavalry Army with Stalin at Tsaritsyn (Stalingrad). This association protected Voroshilov from the consequences of his own mistakes and Stalin's paranoia. He held the position of Commissar for Military and Naval Affairs (renamed Commissar for Defense) from 1925–40. Never known for his intelligence, much of the USSR's ill-preparedness is directly attributed to Voroshilov's incompetence.

Voroshilov did bring new spirit to the Northwest Front when he first arrived. As the situation deteriorated and Stalin contemplated relieving him, the Marshal behaved recklessly at the front, seemingly wanting a hero's death. This was not to be, and in September Zhukov replaced him. Stalin kept him in various high-visibility, but menial, positions until turning against him after the war. Voroshilov fell further from grace during the N.S. Khrushchev era, but L.I. Brezhnev rehabilitated the old marshal.

**Lieutenant General M.M. Popov** commanded the Northern Front from the Arctic Ocean to Leningrad's southern approaches. A former Tsarist colonel, he fought for the Red Army in the Crimea during the Russian Civil War. He is generally credited with steady leadership of his front despite Voroshilov's incompetence. Popov commanded in the Voronezh sector during the German 1942 campaign, an overambitious mobile attack group as part of Operation Saturn, and led the Bryansk Front during the 1943 Kursk battles. He ended the war commanding the 2nd Baltic Front.

**Lieutenant General P.P. Sobennikov** led the 8th Army. In August he took over the Northwest Front when Voroshilov was kicked upstairs to a new position coordinating Leningrad's defense. When the Northwest

Front dissolved, Sobennikov became commander of the 43rd Army defending the northern Moscow area. He survived the war.

In command of the 11th Army was **Lieutenant General V.I. Morozov**. The historian Albert Seaton considered him one of the Red Army's most experienced generals. Morozov contributed to the design of the T-34 tank. Although Barbarossa's opening blows almost annihilated the 11th Army, Morozov managed to maintain it in the field and the 11th was counterattacking near Staraya Russa in 1942.

In the far north, **Lieutenant General V.A. Frolov** commanded the 14th Army (later the Karelian Front) against Dietl's *Gebirgsjäger*. He did such a good job that in 1944 when the time came to take the offensive, Stalin considered Frolov too defensively minded.

Another significant Soviet leader was **Vice Admiral V.F. Tributs**, commanding the Red Banner Baltic Fleet, the Soviet's largest. In contravention of Stalin's orders he took preparatory measures prior to Barbarossa that very likely saved his fleet. As Axis ground forces gobbled up its forward bases, the Baltic fleet was finally trapped on the island base of Kronshtadt. He planned to scuttle the fleet in September but Army Group North ran out of steam before he gave the orders. Tributs commanded the fleet until the end of the war.

# OPPOSING ARMIES

## GERMAN FORCES

Arguably the strength of the German Wehrmacht peaked on 21 June 1941. Although to a lesser degree than its Red Army adversary, it was an army in transition. "Blitzkrieg" is a vague term, understood to mean the combination of mechanization, airpower, flexible command and control using radios, as well as constantly changing objectives. Strategically, Blitzkrieg was episodic, singling out victims sequentially. Since Britain's and America's physical isolation made them less vulnerable to Blitzkrieg tactics, Hitler told von Brauchitsch to disband 35 divisions after the Fall of France, but on 30 June 1940 in fact only stood down 17. Others were reclassified as *Urlaubsdivisionen* (furlough divisions) whose soldiers reported to the war industries.

Subsequent re-expansion negated the army's planned modernization, stretching limited resources. On 21 August Hitler reduced the number of infantry in each panzer division. He also halved the number of panzers in each division, thereby doubling the number of divisions, but never corrected this supposedly temporary expedient. The Führer was confident that 80–100 divisions would be enough to defeat the Red Army. Forty-nine divisions – 29 in Army Group North plus five German and 15 Finnish divisions and three brigades – was too weak a force to achieve German objectives in the north.

Despite the German infantry's prestige, within the Wehrmacht it lost the manpower battle to the SS, Luftwaffe, and *Panzertruppen*. Further

*Landsers* (trans. "those of the land") belonging to the 11th Infantry Division fighting near Dno in August. The steel helmet of the soldier to the left still bears the black-white-red national badge, in theory phased out before Barbarossa. (History in the Making)

A Panzer 38(t) of the 8th Panzer Division near Leningrad. Of a total of 223 panzers, 118 were these near-obsolete Czech models, yet the 8th Panzer represented von Manstein's main striking force. (History in the Making)

dilution occurred when the best infantry divisions were mechanized; with modernization stillborn, the infantry of 1941 looked like that of 1939.

Germany infantry formations were organized along "triangular" lines (a division of three regiments, each with three battalions, etc). Infantry divisions moved at the pace of a marching soldier and a walking horse. Even those infantry in mechanized units that rode to battle fought on foot. Small, hardy *Panje* horses, native to Poland and Russia, met the infantry's logistics needs. Based on observations during the Spanish Civil War, the *Landsers* had learned how to defeat enemy tanks in individual combat. They also possessed the MG34, which the historian, John English calls the "most advanced machine gun of its time."

The new panzers epitomized much of Germany's success during the first part of World War II. In fact Blitzkrieg can be better described as the traditional Prussian/German *Bewegungskrieg* (war of maneuver) wedded to new technology. The Fourth Panzer Group possessed only two panzer corps ("motorized corps") so General Hoepner had difficulty building a *Schwerpunkt.* Panzer divisions usually had two to three panzer battalions, five infantry battalions (four truck mounted, one on motorcycles), and three artillery battalions. Motorized infantry divisions, which often combined with the panzers to create panzer corps, consisted of seven infantry, three to four battalions, and occasionally a panzer battalion.

A panzer battalion usually included three companies of PzKpfw IIIs and one company of PzKpfw IVs. Light panzers, such as the PzKpfw II, were most numerous but had been intended primarily as a stopgap pending the introduction of the PzKpfw III and IV. The *Ostheer* also fielded many captured tanks, including the Czech tank designated PzKpfw 38(t) in German service. They were well-built, reliable and the 38(t) was roughly equivalent to the 37mm PzKpfw III, the 8th Panzer Division having 118 on its order of battle. The older and smaller Skoda 35(t)s were obsolete although the 6th Panzer still possessed 155! Captured French tanks were unsuited to German doctrine and were generally passed on to Germany's allies.

A well-camouflaged 88mm Flak 36/37 gun. Manned by Luftwaffe crews, this weapon could defeat any model of Soviet tank. (History in the Making)

German artillery had been highly developed at the end of the Great War but had not progressed markedly by 1941. One modern innovation was to have forward observers equipped with radios. Mechanized units possessed vehicle-towed or self-propelled artillery pieces, while the indirect fire weapons of infantry divisions were generally horse-drawn. *Nebelwerfer* were demoralizing multi-barreled, anti-personnel weapons, generally found at corps level. Army Group North's super-heavy artillery comprised four "Bruno" (280mm) railroad guns. Anti-tank artillery consisted primarily of 37mm and 50mm caliber guns.

Barbarossa's planners tried unsuccessfully to wish away the monumental logistics problems from the beginning. It is doubtful that if the *Ostheer* had fielded larger forces the German logistics system could have supported them. The internal "divide and conquer" mentality of the Nazis spilled over into this arena. Wehrmacht agencies operated the railroads while the *Grosstransportraum* (figuratively a "bridge" between railroads and units) and the *Aussenstelle* (a higher-level depot system) reported to the Army's Quartermaster General – none accountable to the operational commander. Army Group North was supposed to receive 34 trains of supplies per day but never got more than 18, and achieving even that figure was rare. Non-standard vehicles created a supply and maintenance nightmare; one artillery regiment fielded 69 different vehicle types.

## Waffen SS

In the bizarre polycracy of Nazi Germany fiefdoms competed for power. Around the time of Barbarossa, Reichsführer Heinrich Himmler's personal army eclipsed Göring's Luftwaffe. Two SS divisions fought in Army Group North: "Totenkopf" and "Polizei." "Totenkopf" was essentially a motorized infantry formation. "Polizei," foot infantry, consisted of mobilized policemen. It received recognition as an SS division in 1942. Division "Nord," another *ad hoc* organization, fought in Finland with very uneven results. It was the Army of Norway's only motorized

The 6,700 ton, 6in. gun cruiser *Leipzig* participated in the German operations against the Baltic Islands. Diagonal stripes are often misidentified as "camouflage" but were in reality air-recognition markings for Kriegsmarine ships operating in the Baltic early in the war. (Podzun Verlag)

formation. The 990-man *Einsatzgruppe A* implemented murderous Nazi racial policies behind the front.

## Luftwaffe

The Luftwaffe entered Barbarossa using the same Bf 109s, Ju-52s, Ju-87s and He-111s (with some modifications) as during the Spanish Civil War. Despite the astounding destruction meted out to the Red Air Force during Barbarossa's opening days, the Luftwaffe did not have the strength to fly both air-superiority and close air support missions so the Soviets rapidly bounced back.

The air component in the north, *Luftflotte 1*, was smallest of the three supporting the army groups. *Luftflotte 5* in Norway contributed little considering its huge area of operations. In the north the Red Air Force outnumbered the Luftwaffe nearly 3:1 in bombers, over 7:1 in fighters, and nearly 4:1 overall.

Army Group North only had three Flak regiments assigned. Airborne forces made a brief appearance in the Leningrad area. After recovering from its losses on Crete, the 7th Flieger Division fought on foot around Shlisselburg from mid-September until mid-December.

## Kriegsmarine

While the German Navy's primary mission was to fight the Royal Navy, it had much in common with its Soviet counterpart: both were subordinated to the army and air force; both underwent accelerated development in the 1930s, and both stressed undersea warfare, especially with submarines and mines. Kriegsmarine ships operating in the Baltic usually consisted of three to four light cruisers, five U-Boats, 30–40 fast patrol boats, plus numerous minelayer/sweepers and sub-chasers. The Finns contributed two heavy monitors, four gunboats, five submarines, and six patrol boats. However, coordination between the two navies was weak.

The navy was not fully integrated into the Barbarossa plan; sea transport in the Baltic came as an afterthought and an all-out naval effort was not considered to be necessary. The Germans began mining the Gulfs of Finland and Riga on 12 June. Other Kriegsmarine missions included preventing the Red Banner Fleet from escaping from the Baltic and from launching amphibious operations.

# ORDER OF BATTLE

## Axis Forces*

**NORTHERN THEATER**
**Army of Norway – GenObst Nikolas von Falkenhorst**
*Mountain Corps Norway – Gen MtnTr Eduard Dietl*
2nd Mountain Div. – GenMaj Ernst Schlemmer
3rd Mountain Div. – GenLt Hans Kreysing

*Higher Commando XXXVI – Gen Inf Hans Feige*
169 Inf. Div. – GenMaj Kurt Dittmar
SS-Division "Nord" – SS-Brigadeführer Karl-Maria Demelhuber
6th Div. (Finnish)

**Finnish Army –** Marshal Mannerheim
14th Div. – Col Raapana

**Karelian Army –** GenLt Heinrichs
1st Div. (Res) – Col Paalu
17th Div. – Col Snellman
163rd Inf. Div. (Germ) – GenLt Engelbrecht
Group Oinonen – GenMaj Oinonen
Cavalry Bde. – Col Ehrenrooth
2nd Jäger Bde. – Col Sundman
1st Jäger Bde. (Res) – Col Lagus

*VI Corps – MajGen Talvela*
5th Div. – Col Koskimies
11th Div. – Col Heiskanen

*VII Corps – MajGen Hagglund*
7th Div. – Col Svensson
19th Div. – Col Hannuksela

*II Corps – MajGen Laatikainen*
2nd Div. – Col Blick
15th Div. – Col Hersalo
18th Div. – Col Pajari
10th Div. (Res) – Col Sihvo

*IV Corps – LtGen Oesch*
12th Div. – Col Vihma
4th Div. – Col Viljanen
8th Div. – Col Winell

**ARMY GROUP NORTH**
**GFM Wilhelm *Ritter* von Leeb**

*XXIII Corps – GenInf Albrecht Schubert*
206th Inf. Div. – GenLt Hugo Hoefl
251st Inf. Div. – GenLt Hans Kratzert
254th Inf. Div. – GenLt Walter Behschnitt

*CDR Rear Area 101 – GenLt Franz Roques*
207th Sec Div. – GenLt Karl von Tiedmann
281st Sec Div. – GenLt Friedrich Bayer
285th Sec Div. – GenMaj Wolfgang Elder Herr und Freiherr von Plotho
In transit to the theater:

"Polizei" Division – SS-Gruppenführer Artur Mülverstedt/SS-Obergruppenführer Walter Krüger
86th Inf. Div. – GenLt Joachim Witthoeft

**18th Army – GenObst Georg von Küchler**
291st Inf. Div. – GenLt Kurt Herzog

*I Corps – GenInf Kuno-Hans von Both*
1st Inf. Div. – GenLt Philipp Kleffel
11th Inf. Div. – GenLt Hubert von Boeckmann
21st Inf. Div. – GenLt Otto Sponheimer

*XXVI Corps – GenArt Albert Wodrig*
61st Inf. Div. – GenLt Siegfried Hänicke
217th Inf. Div. – GenLt Richard Baltzer

*XXXVIII Corps – GenInf Fr-Wm von Chappuis*
58th Inf. Div. – GenLt Iwan Heunert

**4th Panzer Group – GenObst Erich Hoepner**
SS-Division "Totenkopf" – SS-Obergruppenführer Theodor Eicke

*XLI Pz. Corps – GenPzTr G-H Reinhardt*
1st Pz. Div. – GenLt Friedrich Kirchner
6th Pz. Div. – GenMaj Franz Landgraf
36th Mot. Inf. Div. – GenLt Otto Ottenbacher
269th Inf. Div. – GenMaj Ernst von Leyser

*LVI Pz. Corps – GenInf Erich von Manstein*
8th Pz. Div. – GenMaj Erich Brandenburger
3rd Mot. Inf. Div. – GenLt Curt Jahn
290th Inf. Div. – GenLt Theodor Freiherr von Wrede

**16th Army – GenObst Ernst Busch**
253rd Inf. Div. – GenLt Otto Schellert

*II Corps – GenInf Walter Graf von Brockdorff-Ahlenfeldt*
12th Inf. Div. – GenMaj Walther von Seydlitz-Kurzbach
32nd Inf. Div. – GenMaj Wilhelm Bohnstedt
121st Inf. Div. – GenMaj Otto Lancelle

*X Corps – GenArt Christian Hansen*
30th Inf. Div. – GenLt Kurt von Tippelskirch
126th Inf. Div. – GenLt Paul Laux

*XXVII Corps – GenInf Mauritz von Wiktorin*
122nd Inf. Div. – GenMaj Siegfried Macholz
123rd Inf. Div. – GenLt Walther Lichel

**Naval Command Group North**

* No two sources on orders of battle for Barbarossa agree. The primary source for the German order of battle is Horst Boog (ed.), *Germany and the Second World War*.

# SOVIET FORCES

At three times the size of the continental United States, the USSR was the world's largest country. While it had the largest army, internal tensions, including the effects of the purges and doctrinal turbulence, almost negated this advantage. Far from being the brittle "colossus of clay" hoped for by the Germans, it survived despite many failings. The Red Army very nearly proved incapable of saving the USSR – it was the Soviet system that held the state together.

Interwar turbulence plagued the Soviet military. Political commissars in military units proved their worth during the Russian Civil War, lost favor in the 1920s, regained influence during the purges, but were again discredited after the Winter War. The Red Army led much of the world in military mechanization through the mid-1930s, but stagnated after the Spanish Civil War only to rebound after watching the Blitzkrieg dismember France. By mid-1940 the Red Army re-established general and admiral ranks and toughened discipline. There became no such thing as a criminal order from above; all orders need to be obeyed accurately, punctually, and without contradiction.

Marshal Tukhachevsky and others stressed the attack. Nevertheless, in the winter of 1939–40 Soviet offensives failed against Finland despite a 5:1 superiority. In the aftermath of the Fall of France and the high-command shake-up of January 1941, Stalin and Zhukov hoped Hitler would not attack until 1942, allowing them to improve the Red Army's defensive capabilities. The official Soviet history states, evidently without irony, "Our prewar theory had not fully worked out the problems of organizing and conducting the defense."

The Northwest Front was the weakest along the main front, initially fielding 369,000 men in 24 divisions and five brigades (the Northern Front contributed a further 19 divisions). Defense Commissar Marshal S.K. Timoshenko and Zhukov had not completed their reforms by *Barbarossatag* so training, organization, and equipment were haphazard.

**Soviet 122mm M1931 guns in action along the Luga line. The Germans took a massive toll on the now-immobile artillery branch, early in the campaign when many prime movers were transferred to the newly raised mechanized corps. (History in the Making)**

The 8th and 11th Armies, their corps and divisions received an order on 26 March to report on their success in implementing MP 41 by 20 June, only two days before Barbarossa began.

The Russian infantryman had a well-earned reputation for toughness, especially in the defense. The Germans noted how they "sat in their slit trenches until they were either run down or killed by hand grenade or bayonet." In the forests common in the north any advantages were magnified; the Germans left their artillery behind and the MG34 lost much of its effectiveness. Here close combat was the rule. Soviet soldiers did not have a scabbard for their bayonet, it was always fixed on their rifle.

Like the standard German infantry formations, Red Army rifle divisions were triangular. Prewar size was 14,483 men but new tables of organization in July reduced this to 10,859 (in reality closer to 6,000). The Northwest Front had an airborne corps of three brigades of four battalions each but it was never used in its intended role.

In contrast to the Germans, Russian artillery performed poorly in the Great War requiring a complete overhaul between the wars. A rifle division included 12 152mm and 20 122mm howitzers and 16 76mm guns, all excellent pieces. Combat losses almost obliterated divisional artillery by July. Most Red Army artillery operated in the direct-support role at corps and division level where it was easier to contol.

Anti-tank weapons were a sub-set of Soviet artillery. They represented the Red Army's preferred weapon to destroy enemy tanks. Guns of 45mm and 57mm size and mines were concentrated in anti-tank brigades. Supposedly motorized, the brigades lost many of their trucks to the new mechanized corps.

Soviet industry produced prodigious numbers of excellent tanks during the interwar years. Many were obsolete by 1941, but were still equal to most German marks while a new generation, led by the T-34, was just arriving on the battlefield. The T-34 epitomized the first true main battle tank, combining anti-tank and infantry-support functions. Even the T-34 had limitations, specifically its weak transmission and two-man turret. The heavy KV-1 mounted the same 76mm gun but its much greater armor weight overtaxed the defective T-34-type transmission. Poor crew skill, maintenance, and supply deprived the Red Army of their potent armored offensive weapon.

The Red Army drew many misguided lessons from the Spanish Civil War, notably identifying tanks as primarily infantry-support weapons. In 1939 they attributed the fall of Poland to the rotten regime, not the Wehrmacht's panzers, with the result that a month later they disbanded the mechanized corps, only to recreate them the following summer in the aftermath of France's defeat. Always thinking "bigger is better," they created huge organizations, way beyond their commanders' ability to manage and lacking any of the panzer corps' flexibility. The Soviets vainly tried to raise 20 new mechanized corps in the six months preceding *Barbarossatag*.

Soviet logistics were arguably in an even worse state than the German. All teeth and no tail meant they had difficulty conducting sustained operations. Much of their logistics base consisted of easily captured or destroyed static dumps. Their mechanized corps, for example, carried only one day's supplies. In the swirling conditions of Barbarossa the Germans easily interdicted soft-skinned supply vehicles.

Out of fuel and often broken down, their tanks became, at best, immobile pillboxes.

### The Red Air Force

Unlike their brothers on the ground, the air force suffered no inferiority complex after their occupation of Poland or the Winter War. However, the Red Air Force's effectiveness had also peaked in the 1930s and by 1941 it was growing obsolete. Many veterans of the Spanish Civil War had been framed and arrested during the purges. The paucity of radios mirrored that of the army. Soviet aviators stubbornly retained the ineffective, three-plane "V" formation.

The Red Air Force came out fighting, many planes flying 10–14 sorties on 22 June. In the Soviet leadership vacuum that day (and for many more days) regimental commanders improvised by sending their men against any target. They made little effort to evade German fighters or flak. But total German losses that day of 78 aircraft exceeded their worst day during the Battle of Britain (61 aircraft on 15 September 1940).

### Soviet Navy

The Red Banner Baltic Fleet had great potential on 21 June. It had a competent leader in Admiral Tributs and two battleships, two light cruisers, 47 destroyers or large torpedo boats, 75 submarines, and over 200 smaller craft and hundreds of aircraft. Outnumbering the Kriegsmarine, it nevertheless relied mainly on mines and submarines.

Unfortunately, the loss of all but one naval base and a passive doctrine meant the Red Banner Fleet did not realize its potential. It did survive, however, and in May 1945 it, not the Kriegsmarine, was the victor. In the Arctic Ocean the Northern Fleet was more active, often with the assistance of the Royal Navy.

# ORDER OF BATTLE

## Soviet Forces*

**NORTHERN FRONT**
LtGen M.M. Popov

177th Rifle Division
191st Rifle Division
8th Rifle Brigade

**Northern PVO – MajGen Protsvetkin**
39th Fighter Aviation Division
3rd Fighter Aviation Division (PVO)
54th Fighter Aviation Division (PVO)
2nd Mixed Aviation Division

**14th Army – LtGen V.A. Frolov**
14th Rifle Division
52nd Rifle Division
1st Tank Division

1st Mixed Aviation Division

*42nd Rifle Corps – MajGen R.I. Panin*
104th Rifle Division
122nd Rifle Division

**7th Independent Army – LtGen F.D. Gorelenko**
54th Rifle Division
71st Rifle Division
168th Rifle Division
237th Rifle Division

55th Mixed Aviation Division

**23rd Army – MajGen P.S. Pshennikov**
*19th Rifle Corps – MajGen M.N. Gerasimov*
115th Rifle Division
142nd Rifle Division

*50th Rifle Corps – MajGen V.I. S'cherbakov*
43rd Rifle Division
70th Rifle Division
123rd Rifle Division

*10th Mechanized Corps – MajGen I.G. Lazarev*
21st Tank Division
24th Tank Division
198th Motorcycle Division
7th Motorcycle Regiment

41st Bomber Aviation Division
5th Mixed Aviation Division

**NORTHWEST FRONT**
ColGen F.I. Kuznetsov

*5th Airborne Corps – MajGen I.S. Berugly*
9th Airborne Brigade
10th Airborne Brigade
214th Airborne Brigade

**Baltic VVS – MajGen A. Ionov**
57th Fighter Aviation Division
4th Mixed Aviation Division
6th Mixed Aviation Division
7th Mixed Aviation Division
8th Mixed Aviation Division

9th Anti-tank Brigade

**8th Army – LtGen P.P. Sobennikov**
*10th Rifle Corps – MajGen I.F. Nikolaev*
10th Rifle Division
48th Rifle Division
50th Rifle Division

*11th Rifle Corps – MajGen M.S. Shurnilov*
11th Rifle Division
125th Rifle Division

*12th Mechanized Corps – MajGen N.M. Shestopalov*
23rd Tank Division
202nd Mechanized Division
10th Motorcycle Regiment

**11th Army – LtGen V.I. Morozov**
23rd Rifle Division
126th Rifle Division
128th Rifle Division

*16th Rifle Corps – MajGen F.S. Ivanov*
5th Rifle Division
33rd Rifle Division
188th Rifle Division

*29th Rifle Corps – MajGen A.G. Samokhin*
179th Rifle Division
184th Rifle Division

*3rd Mechanized Corps – MajGen A.V. Kurkin*
2nd Tank Division
5th Tank Division
84th Mechanized Division

**27th Army – MajGen M.E. Berzarin**
16th Rifle Division
76th Rifle Division
3rd Rifle Brigade

*22nd Rifle Corps – MajGen M.P. Dukhanov*
180th Rifle Division
182nd Rifle Division

*24th Rifle Corps – MajGen K. Kachalov*
181st Rifle Division
183rd Rifle Division

**Red Banner Baltic Fleet – Vice Adm V.F. Tributs
Northern Fleet – Rear Adm Gorlovko**

*As with the Axis order of battle, sources conflict on the details of Red Army organization. The primary source for the Soviet order of battle is David Glantz, *Barbarossa*.

# OPERATION BARBAROSSA

## FRONTIER BATTLES

On 22 April von Leeb's headquarters moved from Dresden to Waldfrieden, barely 50 miles from Hitler's *Wolfschanze*. This proximity did not engender conceptual closeness between the two men. On 30 May regimental commanders received their attack orders. Officers in troop units still spoke of "bluff" and "demonstration" against the USSR and an invasion of Great Britain instead. Reality intruded at 1300hrs on 21 June when Army Group North received the codeword "Düsseldorf," indicating Barbarossa would start the next morning, and passed down its own codeword "Dortmund."

Surprise attacks, without declarations of war, were central to Soviet military theory. Yet one hour before the Germans' artillery preparation, Red Army High Command signaled its armies: "No provocations will be made which could lead to complications … Meet a German surprise attack with all forces available." Stalin might have been worried about "victory-drunk German generals" but seemed more concerned about not provoking a war than preparing for one.

### Panzer Thrust to the Dvina River

Von Leeb's units moved into jumping-off positions in the crowded Memelland on 18 June. Leaders reconnoitered the front dressed as East Prussian farmers. At around 0345hrs on 22 June their artillery

A pair of the 30 Panzer IVs in the 8th Panzer Division advancing through Lithuania. Each pulls a trailer with extra fuel, perhaps suggesting that the supply lines were already feeling the strain. The exposed position of both tank commanders indicates that they are not expecting action. (History in the Making)

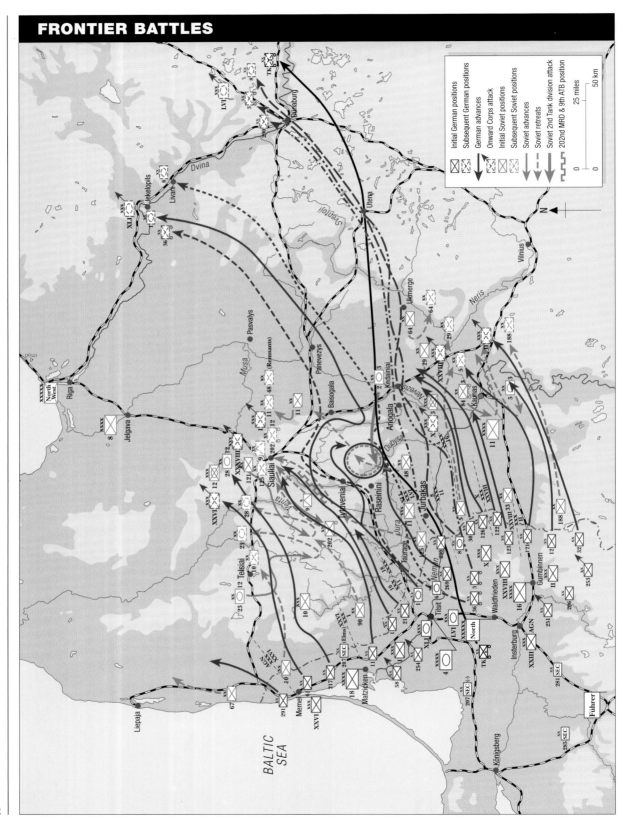

Briefing armored car crewmen of the 12th Mechanized Corps during the battles against the XLI Panzer Corps at Raseiniai. Parked in the tree line are BA-6 or BA-10 scout cars. (History in the Making)

preparation began, lasting between 45 minutes and three hours. Irregular Soviet artillery defensive fire began within an hour, followed by Red Air Force attacks a further hour later, both indicating at least a degree of preparedness. Thick fog confused the situation until about 0500hrs and advancing *Landsers* immediately encountered the swamps and marshes that characterized the campaign in the north. Although Kuznetsov defended with only one regiment per division forward, already on the first day older officers noted they faced "a different enemy than in 1914."

Long days and short nights meant hard marching and fighting, and little rest for either side. On 22 June the 291st Infantry Division advanced 40 miles, while the 8th Panzer Division covered nearly 50 miles to capture a crossing of the Dubysa River's deep ravine at Ariogala. In some locations Soviet defenders fought bitterly, elsewhere the Germans reported "the enemy is not to be seen." It took 18 days for Stavka (created on 23 June) to receive a situation report from the Northwest Front. Stalin's high command ordered Königsberg and Memel bombed, and the 3rd and 12th Mechanized Corps to occupy attack positions. Kuznetsov was relatively lucky that he faced only one panzer group. However, his 2nd Tank Division (which included 55 T-34 and KV tanks out of a total of 200, but was separated from the remainder of the 3rd Mechanized Corps) missed the 8th Panzer Division like two ships passing in the night.

German intelligence misinterpreted the enemy's retreat as a general withdrawal. The Soviets had different plans. On the morning of 23 June, Sobennikov ordered the 3rd Mechanized Corps to attack northwest and the 12th Mechanized Corps to advance southeast by noon. To get to their assembly areas the 3rd and 12th Mechanized Corps marched 60 and 50 miles respectively; both corps had less than one and a half hours to prepare. Therefore Soviet counterattacks began slowly on the 23rd, but intensified over the next two days.

Sobennikov's target, the XLI Panzer Corps, was spread out. The 1st Panzer Division fought its way through Taurage, where the Soviets had turned every building into a small fort. By the evening of 23 June, with

A medic attends to a wounded soldier fighting in the Dünaburg bridgehead in late June. The capture of the bridge after just four days represented a major coup for von Manstein although his men then had to fight hard to hold it. (History in the Making)

the assistance of the Brandenburger's *Wachkompanie,* 1st Panzer captured a critical 300-yard-long railroad bridge at Tytuvenai. The 6th Panzer Division outran its logistical support on the first day and desperately needed ammunition. The division failed to achieve its initial mission, another Dubysa crossing, and now assumed an *Igel* (hedgehog) defense near Raseiniai as over 100 Red Army tanks struck. Its motorcycle infantry battalion survived 20 minutes. General Reinhardt sensed danger, and ordered the 1st Panzer to halt and turn east in support. Panzers and KV-1s engaged at ranges of 30–60 yards. Sunlight illuminated the slaughter for 18 hours a day.

The XLI Panzer Corps battled to save its spearhead. With its PzKpfw 35(t)s the 6th Panzer Division appeared isolated and overwhelmed. The 2nd Tank Division smashed the 114th Motorized Infantry Regiment, crushing vehicles and mutilating German wounded and POWs. For the first time in the accompanying infantry divisions, the cry went out "*Panzerjäger* to the front!"

The 25th was the critical day of the armor battle. Soviet tanks and infantry ambushed the 1st Panzer Division's command post, where General Kirchner and his staff defended themselves with their individual weapons. However Kuznetsov forfeited mass and concentration by ordering his mechanized formations to "operate in small columns to avoid enemy aircraft." The 1st Panzer made slow progress through the sand and moorland, but soon arrived to help the 6th. Together these two units averted the crisis and actually trapped much of the 3rd Mechanized Corps; the 12th Mechanized Corps was destroyed soon after.

The 12th Mechanized Corps mustered 690 tanks on 22 June. A week later it counted 50 operational tanks. Tanks that ran out of fuel became pillboxes, which German sappers had to take out in difficult and time-consuming individual actions. *I Fliegerkorps* claimed over 200 tanks were destroyed on the Raseiniai battlefield. The historian David Glantz considers the Soviet 28th Tank Division's losses of 198 out of 220 tanks

Exhausted German soldiers relax in the shade of a building. Unusually, the men appear to wear SS-pattern camouflaged helmet covers and smocks over their regular army tunics. (History in the Making)

typical. Now free to advance, and with a contingent of Brandenburger commandos, the 1st Panzer Division gained its own Dvina bridgehead at Jekolopils to bring it up alongside with the LVI Panzer Corps.

Army Group North achieved greater success with von Manstein's rush to the critical Dvina crossing at Dünaburg. After seizing the bridge at Ariogala, his three divisions stretched along a single road like an "armored centipede." In 100 hours they covered 200 miles, the same distance as from the German border to Dunkirk. Luftwaffe reconnaissance could see no enemy forces to their front. The LVI Panzer Corps exploited an 80-mile gap created when the Sixteenth Army and Hermann Hoth's Third Panzer Group pushed the 11th Army east, instead of north with the remainder of Kuznetsov's Front.

Hoepner's Panzers had not been associated with an infantry army, primarily so they could race for Dünaburg unencumbered. Kuznetsov ordered the 27th Army, augmented by the 21st Mechanized Corps, to make for the fortified city but von Manstein got there first. A flying column, led by Brandenburgers riding in captured Soviet trucks followed by pioneers and the 29th Panzergrenadier Regiment, streaked across Latvia in the early morning of 26 June, watched passively by awakening Red Army soldiers. By 0800hrs, first the Brandenburgers then the other German elements arrived at 15–20 minute intervals capturing one vehicle- and one railroad bridge. The Soviets attempted to torch the latter, but were thwarted by German pioneers.

Kuznetsov initiated counterattacks in the evening of 27 June. Though *Landsers* marched quickly to close the 75-mile gap, for three days the isolated LVI Panzer Corps' only outside assistance came from Luftwaffe close air support. The Red Air Force flew 2,100 sorties against von Manstein's men, and the Luftwaffe Bf 109s of *Jagdgeschwader 54* went on a killing spree. *Zerstörergeschwader 26* alone destroyed over 200 tanks.

On 25 June, Timoshenko ordered Kuznetsov to hold the Dvina, but he failed to do so. To compound the error of allowing the 11th Army to slip eastward from the border battles toward Opochka, Kuznetsov now ordered the remnants of the 27th Army to do the same. If giving the

**SOVIET 8TH ARMY ATTEMPTS TO BREAK OUT THROUGH LVI PANZER CORPS, DÜNABURG BRIDGEHEAD, 28 JUNE 1941** (pages 36–37)

The Germans considered the Dvina–Dnepr River line the Red Army's last, best hope at halting Barbarossa early. If their panzers could rush the rivers and establish bridgeheads on the far bank they believed they could unhinge the Soviets' defenses and prevent an 1812-style withdrawal. In Army Group North's area the Dvina bridges at Dünaburg stood tantalizingly close to the Nazi–Soviet frontier. General Hoepner calculated that his panzers could conduct such a daring "panzer raid." With speed and flexibility in mind his Panzer Group Four was not subordinated to an infantry army. General von Manstein's LVI Panzer Corps had the mission of *Schwerpunkt* for this raid. For their part the Soviets were not prepared for the coming onslaught. They assumed German forces in East Prussia and the Government General would make generally for Moscow. General Kuznetsov's Northwest Front initially did not have sufficient forces to hold Field Marshal von Leeb. Kuznetsov's weak leadership compounded this problem as it withdrew from the border: his 8th Army pulled back due north and the 11th Army retreated toward the east with the Western Front. These moves, made without a firm hand from above, opened the road to Dünaburg to von Manstein's men. On the morning of Barbarossa's fourth day a motorized infantry task force plus a company of Brandenburg commandos sped past Soviets too stunned to react. Red Army soldiers guarding the bridges failed to halt the Germans, could not respond effectively, and the Germans held Dünaburg's three bridges after a matter of minutes.

(1) Teutonic Knights founded Dünaburg in 1278, but the massive seventeenth-century brick fortress faced toward invaders from Germany. (2) It was from this direction that Kuznetsov's escaping men came. First von Manstein's 8th Panzer then the 3rd Motorized Divisions occupied Dünaburg and now held the bridgehead. Soviet soldiers from the 21st Mechanized and 5th Airborne Corps trickled north to escape the pursuing Germans, not realizing the LVI Panzer Corps barred the way. Soon elements of the 27th Army's 16th Rifle Corps, belatedly sent to fill the Dünaburg gap, were trapped as well. Overhead the 8th Mixed and 61st Fighter Brigades sought to destroy the bridges and help their comrades on the ground. Bf 109s of JG 53 Pik As and JG 54 Gruenherz created a holocaust of Red Air Force aircraft, shooting down 74 planes in one day. Members of 8th Panzer established a hasty defense as desperate Soviets pressed against them. German heavy weapons from the fortress fired down in support. (3) Soviets picked their way forward, in this case with a Maxim 1911 machine gun (4), trying to fight their way to the bridge and hopefully, re-establish a valid defense of their homeland. Here a Panzer Mark II has been destroyed by a shot to the turret (5). The battlefield is littered with death and destruction and the sky is criss-crossed with the smoke of falling Soviet airplanes (6). Unfortunately for the Red Army men their efforts were too disjointed and the Germans too well entrenched. Although many made it across the river, they did not reinstate a legitimate defense. However, neither could von Leeb exploit the brightest spot in Barbarossa's opening few days; he thought and acted too slowly to exploit von Manstein's gains. (Peter Dennis)

Germans a clear run to Dünaburg were not bad enough, he had now opened the road to Leningrad. On 29 June, Stavka instructed him to defend the Stalin Line, another mission in which he would fail. Stalin relieved Kuznetsov and his political officer the next day for having "failed to organize a stable front."[1] Sobennikov was promoted to command of the front, and General F.S. Ivanov in turn took command of the 8th Army. Most significantly, the Northwest Front received a new and energetic chief of staff, tasked to master the situation "at all cost" and halt the Germans, Lieutenant General N.F. Vatutin.

**Infantry Armies on the Flanks**

As Eighteenth Army advanced through the Baltic states, elements of its 291st Infantry Division neared Liepaja, ably defended by the 67th Rifle Division on Barbarossa's second day. The 11th Infantry Division fought over trenches and fortifications dating from 1915–17. Siauliai fell on 26 June. Ventspils was soon flying a white flag and the 61st Infantry Division, destined to play crucial roles in the story of this campaign, crossed the Dvina on 30 June to capture Riga against minimal resistance a day later. Von Küchler's men covered over 150 miles in ten days. To avoid marching in the worst of the heat, von Küchler often limited movement to 0300–0800hrs and 1800–2200hrs.

By now surrounded on three sides by Fourth Panzer Group and the Eighteenth Army, Soviet 8th Army was threatened with destruction. Both I and XXVI Infantry Corps amalgamated all their trucks with their assault guns to create fast detachments in an attempt to encircle the 8th Army. Von Küchler led from the front but after three days he feared his small groups would be crushed by the mass of Soviet troops and slowed the chase; the Soviets escaped the parallel pursuit.

The Sixteenth Army tried to stay close to Hoepner, cover von Leeb's eastern flank, and maintain contact with Army Group Center. Within two days its 121st Infantry Division reached the fortress city of Kaunas, Lithuanian capital, and 11th Army headquarters. Red Army defenders had destroyed Neman and Neris river bridges but X Corps engineers rebuilt them by 25 June. The Soviets launched fierce counterattacks on the 26th and General Busch's men used every infantry weapon at their disposal plus assault guns and Lithuanian "activists" to hold their bridgehead.

The Sixteenth Army then maintained the pursuit through two weeks of heat and dust interrupted by an occasional day of rain. Marching was tough but morale remained high. Brandenburgers captured 24 intact bridges throughout the army's area. By the night of 3–4 July the 30th Infantry Division captured Busch's first crossing of the Dvina near Livani. The II Corps fell in behind Hoepner's panzers. The Sixteenth Army relied on aerial resupply and captured Soviet stocks as late as mid-July due to convoy interdiction by Red Army groups still operating behind German lines.

However, a major concern of Army Group North (and Halder) was the boundary with von Bock. Busch dedicated an entire corps to maintaining contact with the Ninth Army. This became more difficult when the Ninth veered south to the Bialystok *Kessel* (pocket). As the two army groups

---

**1** From the official Soviet history, *History of the Great Patriotic War of the Soviet Union, 1941–45*

A German soldier inspects a Soviet sniper's nest high in a tree. Snipers were such a threat in the heavily wooded north that the SS-Divison "Totenkopf" commander Theodor Eicke authorized division officers to remove rank insignia on Barbarossa's second day. (History in the Making)

diverged toward individual objectives the gap widened and became more dangerous. By 4 July Halder noted threatening Soviet movement to Velikie Luki, "between Hoth and Hoepner."

\* \* \*

On 24 June von Leeb enthusiastically wrote in his diary that von Manstein's Dünaburg bridgehead represented "A stake into the heart of the enemy." Hoepner's motto was "Surprise, then forward, forward, forward." Reinhardt wondered when the unified panzers would hit the Soviets. However, Hoepner's superiors never allowed the panzer group to fight as more than two separate corps. From the start LVI Panzer Corps raced for Dünaburg while the XLI Panzer Corps fought for its life against the bulk of two mechanized corps. This disastrous trend continued beyond Leningrad. Toward the Baltic Sea coast the Eighteenth Army was too weak and too thinly spread to spring a trap on the Soviet 8th Army. Inland Sixteenth Army was unable to establish a solid link with Army Group Center.

Overhead, in three days *I Fliegerkorps* flew 1,600 sorties, bombed 77 airfields, shot down 400 aircraft, and destroyed a further 1,100 on the ground. By 25 June there were no more Red Air Force bases to attack and evidently few aircraft left to destroy. The Luftwaffe had little choice but to change missions from air superiority to close air support. On the ground *Landsers* griped of re-equipped Soviet flyers but Luftwaffe generals complained about being nothing more than aerial artillery.

During the border battles, Kuznetsov lost 1,444 tanks and armored vehicles, nearly 4,000 guns, 90,000 men killed, but "only" 35,000 captured. He failed to defend his sector and lost his job. The six-day pause to allow Busch to catch up with Hoepner killed Army Group North's momentum and allowed the Northwest Front to avoid destruction. On 29 June Hitler told his OKW Chief, Field Marshal Wilhelm Keitel, to "concentrate Hoepner's panzers at Dünaburg … and drive through Ostrov." Both von Brauchitsch and von Leeb disagreed and did all they could to delay the panzers. Their willfulness and caution put "a stake into the heart" of their own chances of victory.

## THE DRIVE NORTH

Von Leeb violated every tenet of the Blitzkrieg when he halted Hoepner for six days on the Dvina. Furthermore, he kept the already too small panzer group from concentrating. Neither Führer Directive 18 nor the *Aufmarschanweisung* firmly stated whether von Leeb should aim directly for Leningrad or veer northeast so he could attack either Leningrad or Moscow – Halder's pet project. The OKH maintained tighter control over Fourth Panzer Group than its contemporaries because of its "danger of being encircled and destroyed in the vast forests in front of Leningrad unless it has the support of closely-following infantry divisions."[2]

On the Soviet side, the average strength of a Northwest Front rifle division shrank to about 2,000 men. As their tanks melted away the Red Army created nothing larger than tank brigades. By the end of June the

Soviets knew they had lost their first echelon. In response, they did add 30 small (3,447 troopers) but mobile cavalry divisions. Following *Barbarossatag*, the Soviets managed to mobilize nine new armies in June, 13 in July, and 15 in August. Aware Kuznetsov had made a mess of his Front's defense, on 2 July Stavka instructed the Northern Front to re-orient Leningrad's efforts toward the south and the Luga River. The burden of the defense would fall on the Luga Operational Group (LOG), holding the river line between Narva and Lake Il'men.

Having decided to defend Leningrad along the Luga, Northern Front commander Popov sent his deputy General K.P. Piadyshev to survey a possible defense line there. On 9 July, Piadyshev took command of the LOG, consisting at first of two rifle and three militia divisions (DNOs 1, 2 and 3, created by the Leningrad Military Soviet five days earlier) and a mountain brigade. He later received four more rifle divisions and the 21st and 24th Tank Divisions. Behind this line stood two more defensive lines reaching back to Leningrad's suburbs. The scene was set for the battle for the USSR's second city.

At Führer Headquarters near swampy Lake Mauer, Hitler came down with dysentery and stomach pains and suffered through much of July and half of August. While his personal physician, Dr Theo Morell, pumped the dictator full of medications, a crisis of command paralyzed the *Ostheer's* decision making. Von Brauchitsch, Halder and others took full advantage of this leadership vacuum to push their own agendas and hamstring Barbarossa.

### The Stalin Line

With his army group temporarily consolidated, until the panzers again outpaced the infantry, von Leeb instructed his men to resume the advance in early July. Leading the XLI Panzer Corps, the 1st Panzer Division advanced 70 miles on 2 July against weak Soviet resistance to a point only 30 miles from Ostrov. Although Red Army efforts seemed to be directed against the LVI Panzer Corps coming up from Rezekne,

A Soviet cavalry formation belonging to the 11th Army seen near Dünaburg in June. Following tremendous tank losses the Red Army reverted to cavalry for mobility until sufficient new armored forces could be created. (History in the Making)

Traffic jam at a Luga River bridge in late August. The river is neither wide, with steep banks, nor fast flowing yet was obviously an obstacle. German pioneers have constructed a new bridge to the left. (History in the Making)

Hoepner would not allow dilution of Reinhardt's advance in order to help von Manstein.

Just ahead of the 27th Army, the 1st Panzer Division took Ostrov on 4 July, clearing its railroad bridge by 1730hrs. The 27th Army immediately counterattacked and soon the entire town was in flames. With Red Air Force, close air support, and KV tanks the Soviets renewed their assaults on 8 July. By noon the Germans' situation was desperate and they fell back into the relative safety of the burning town. As Reinhardt's men stabilized the situation, 100 burning enemy tanks illuminated the night. New, well-coordinated Soviet attacks began at 0300hrs on 11 July. However, the Red Army units were spent, and the panzers renewed their advance the next day. The Luftwaffe flew 1,200 sorties, and claimed 140 tanks and 112 aircraft destroyed during the Velikaya bridgehead battles. By 10 July Red Air Force elements counted only 102 aircraft from an original 1,142. With the old bunkers of the former Latvian–Russian border behind them Hoepner's men had turned the vaunted Stalin Line. The 27th Army retreated east through the swamps toward Opochka with von Manstein in pursuit.

Von Küchler had previously isolated remnants of the 8th Army but the latter now manned the Parnu–Tartu line. The 61st Infantry Division briefly held Tartu, but did not have sufficient ammunition to maintain its position. By 13 July the 61st occupied an *Igel* south of Poltsamaa against the 10th Rifle Corps. Further inland *Landsers* finally caught up to the fight after weeks of marching 20–30 miles day after day. The Sixteenth Army fought the fresh 22nd Army from Dno to Polozk. With the Soviets mounting a serious defense, combat in the unusual terrain required new tactics. Communications with neighboring units was difficult and large gaps existed between formations.

\* \* \*

Now in Russia proper, the wilderness and the impoverished conditions of the people stunned the Germans. By 6 July von Manstein was stuck in the swamps near Opochka. Confusion reigned within Army Group headquarters as von Leeb, Hoepner, and von Manstein argued over the direction LVI Panzer Corps should take: reinforce Reinhardt or strike out on its own toward Staraya Russa. On the 10th von Leeb remarked in his diary "the Russians defend every step." It took von Manstein's men until the night of 10/11 July to capture Opochka, only to be subjected to immediate counterattacks. Hoepner wanted to swing north to trap Red Army forces facing the Eighteenth Army west of Lake Peipus. Miserable terrain, Red Army defenders employing minefields, abatis, and other obstacles slowed the operation. The XLI Panzer Corps, using the primitive roads, reached the Plyussa River on 12 July. Luftwaffe air attacks failed to halt the Soviet's continued withdrawal.

As early as 30 June Hitler toyed with the idea of sending two panzer groups (Hoepner and Hoth) first to Leningrad and then to Moscow. This plan might have worked, but by 4 July he still had not made the decision. After squandering nine irreplaceable days and thinking the Soviets were beaten, on 8 July Hitler and Halder agreed Third Panzer Group would not participate against Leningrad. On 9 July, von Brauchitsch, von Leeb, and Hoepner met at Army Group headquarters and hammered out a compromise with regard to Fourth Panzer Group's actual method. Both of Hoepner's Panzer Corps would make for the massive city, XLI via Pskov and the lower Luga, LVI through Novgorod. The Sixteenth Army would cover Hoepner's exposed right while the Eighteenth would clear the Baltic states and follow Reinhardt. This plan lasted only four days; by 13 July the issue was not whether Hoth would support von Leeb, but whether his panzer group would go all the way to Leningrad or only so far as Velikie Luki.

Around this time Stalin made some leadership changes of his own. The Soviets created a new echelon of command, the Strategic Direction. Directions came from the World War I tradition and were not independent staffs but an extension of Stavka under a marshal. On 10 July Marshal K.E. Voroshilov arrived to coordinate the efforts of the Northern and Northwest Fronts plus the Northern and Red Banner Fleets. Voroshilov may have been a trusted crony of Stalin's but could not lead; his Northwest Direction would be the first to go on 30 August. On 15 July the Red Army temporarily disbanded rifle corps as superfluous. In any event it no longer had sufficient staffs to man those that remained.

## Into Russia

The area between Lakes Peipus and Il'men and south of Petersburg is the historical Ingermannland. It marked the boundary between the Russians and first the Teutonic Knights, and later the Baltic states. Sixteenth Army and Fourth Panzer Group fought here until the end of August. Logistics, sanguinely sidestepped during most of Barbarossa's planning, now dominated operations. It is appropriate to quote Martin van Creveld at length: "In the second half of July the supply service was incapable of supporting even the most limited offensive because it was fully occupied moving its base forward from Dünaburg to the area around Luga, and in this period the start of the attack was postponed no fewer than seven times … The offensive was resumed on 8 August but by that time the defense of Leningrad was ready."

Less than 24 hours into the German invasion, Popov began looking south at the axis of attack along the Pskov highway. His commissar,

Half-tracks, Sturmgeschütze, and other vehicles of the LVI Panzer Corps in the open terrain characteristic of Barbarossa's early weeks. Once past the Velikaya River von Manstein's lightning advances fell foul of more difficult terrain. (US National Archives)

A.A. Zhandov soon had 200,000 civilians digging hundreds of miles of anti-tank ditches and trenches, creating 15,000 fighting positions and 22 miles of barricades in front of Leningrad. Fearing the worst, authorities evacuated two thirds of a million civilians from the city by August.

Reinhardt advanced on the left as planned along the highway toward Luga with the XXXVIII Army Corps behind. Hoepner's second *coup de main* in capturing a critical bridgehead came in early July near Kingisepp. The 1st and 6th Panzer Divisions raced north on roughly parallel courses east of Lake Peipus. A *Kampfgruppe* including Brandenburger commandos under Colonel Erhard Raus worked its way through forest and marsh to a bridge at Ivanovskoye early on 14 July. His men discovered the bridge unguarded plus another bridge not on their maps. Farther south at Sabsk, the 1st Panzer Division likewise secured a bridgehead. The Soviets rushed reinforcements directly to the threatened area on trains from Leningrad. Many were militia units that achieved little. Until 19 August Reinhardt's men relied exclusively on Luftwaffe resupply.

The XLI Panzer Corps had fought across 650 miles in less than one month and Leningrad was fewer than 100 miles away. However, despite having crossed the last major river barrier before the city, Leningrad itself would prove beyond XLI Panzer Corps' reach. While the Red Army dug a network of obstacles, trenches and bunkers to their front, Reinhardt's men settled into a relatively costly defensive battle. His panzer raid reaped no great operational benefits as von Manstein had earlier, or as Model would later at Novgorod Severskiy (see Campaign 129 *Operation Barbarossa 1941 (1) Army Group South*). On 27 July, an exasperated Reinhardt tried in vain to resign, saying "This [wait] is dreadful ... the decisive opportunity [to rush Leningrad] has passed."

To the southeast the LVI Panzer Corps hacked its way through the wilderness between Opochka and Novgorod. Limited to one major road von Manstein's troops stretched out in a long line, 60 miles from Reinhardt and over 50 miles from the marching infantry behind. The situation was worse for Kuznetsov, however. On 10 July Stavka told him of its "absolute dissatisfaction with the work of the Northwest Front," saying commanders at every echelon "have not fulfilled our orders and like criminals have abandoned their defensive positions." By mid-month Piadyshev had been arrested. Stavka subsequently divided the 250-mile long Luga defenses into three parts, each commanded by a major general: Kingisepp under V.V. Semashko, Luga (town) under A.N. Astanin, and Eastern under F.N. Starikov.

Von Manstein's thrust aimed initially for Novgorod with a subsequent objective of cutting the Moscow–Leningrad rail line at Chudovo. Taking advantage of the Germans' vulnerable isolation, and perhaps spurred by Stavka's criticism, the 11th Army struck the LVI Panzer Corps near Soltsy. With the supporting I Army Corps far to the rear, Vatutin's forces fought a desperate battle from 14–18 July. The northern arm of the attack consisted mainly of the 10th Mechanized Corps, and the southern of the 16th and 22nd Rifle Corps. They cut off 8th Panzer Division, the vanguard, from the rest of LVI Panzer Corps which, surrounded in marshy terrain, could not maneuver on the narrow corduroy roads.

Over a two-day period 3rd Motorized and "Totenkopf" fought their way forward to rescue the 8th Panzer. By the time von Manstein stabilized the situation 8th Panzer Division had lost 70 of its 150 operational panzers. Von Manstein required four days to save General Brandenburger's division while Hoepner diverted resources from the XLI Panzer Corps' successful operations to assist. The attack left the 8th Panzer Division severely shaken, and in any event Hoepner soon transferred it to Reinhardt.

Von Leeb again insisted his forces halt and clean up the situation before continuing. He therefore detached von Manstein's most powerful formation, the recently rescued 8th Panzer while over half of Busch's army secured the boundary with Army Group Center. Still, most of his supplies had to be flown in due to Red Army stragglers and now partisans in the Sixteenth Army's rear area.

Another crisis mastered, von Manstein continued to the Luga River with the 3rd Motorized, "Totenkopf" and 269th Infantry Divisions. Hitler, and indeed the OKH, insisted this thrust be Hoepner's *Schwerpunkt*. They agreed on the need to send Hoepner's right-hand corps on a great counterclockwise arc to cut off Leningrad from Moscow and affect a junction with the Finns at the Svir. Beginning on 24 July, and with *Nebelwerfer* support, the LVI Panzer Corps fought slowly forward against determined defenders. The Soviets inflicted numerous losses and more than once von Manstein pulled his men back to their starting positions, but by 2 August he was ready to assault the town of Luga.

South of Lake Il'men *Landsers* of the 30th Infantry Division resorted to flamethrowers, bayonets, and hand-to-hand combat to inch forward in the face of the Soviets' tenacious defense. In front of the 30th Infantry Division, near Staraya Russa, Luftwaffe reconnaissance noted a defensive system of trenches, mines, and barbed wire many miles deep. To their left the 121st Infantry Division prepared to attack near Utogorsh. Von Richthofen's *VIII Fliegerkorps* (four Stuka and three fighter *Gruppen*) arrived to help. Weather delayed D-Day three times in four days. Artillery could not destroy Soviet bunkers buried beneath six feet of soil. In two days 121st Infantry Division casualties exceeded a third of those suffered during Barbarossa's first five weeks. Division headquarters issued "General Instructions #4" that concluded the enemy's talents "can be a remarkable example to us."

**Voroshilov's political closeness to Stalin did not equate to military skill. First Kuznetsov then Voroshilov made such a hash of defending Leningrad's southern approaches as to almost guarantee German success. (David Glantz)**

Soviet 45mm M1937 anti-tank gunners come under fire near Pskov in early July. These 11th Army soldiers had been conducting a fighting withdrawal without effective command from above, falling back in front of von Leeb's men rather than halting them. (History in the Making)

### The Fall of Tallinn

The weak Eighteenth Army struggled up the strategic Baltic Sea littoral against an even weaker 8th Army. With effective Red Air Force close air support, the 16th Rifle Division defended Tartu ably while the 11th Rifle held Viljandi. Frustrated at the delay, on 21 July Army Group headquarters ordered the Eighteenth Army to attack with the XXVI Army Corps the next day. At 0300hrs, exactly one month after Barbarossa's start, the 61st Infantry Division and *Sturmgeschütz Abteilung 185* assaulted Poltsamaa. A day later the 217th Infantry attacked at Turi and by the evening of 25 July these two units had trapped most of the 48th and 125th Rifle Divisions against Lake Peipus, capturing over 9,000 POWs. The XXVI Corps kept up the pressure and by 8 August its 245th Infantry Division reached the Gulf of Finland at Kunda.

Intent on depriving the Red Banner Fleet of its last base outside Kronshtadt, the Germans planned to reduce Tallinn. Under overall command of Admiral Tributs, but tactically led by the 10th Corps (two rifle and two mechanized divisions under Major General I.F. Nikolaev), 20,000 soldiers and 25,000 civilians prepared the defense. From west to east Nikolaev stationed the 22nd Motorized, 16th Rifle, and 10th Motorized Divisions backed up by marines. The Soviets expected the main effort to come from the south, but the German *Schwerpunkt* was to the east.

The XLII Infantry Corps attacked at 0330hrs on 20 August with the 217th, 61st, and 254th Infantry Divisions (west to east) supported by 210mm mortars and assault guns. Estonian "Self Defense Forces" kept the German rear areas safe from partisans. Red Army defenders put up tough resistance but by 27 August the Germans reached Tallinn's outskirts. The 61st entered the city a day later, marching single file over miles of railroad embankments. Tributs had evacuated most of the garrison except for an 11,000-man rearguard on the night of 27 August. Nearly 190 vessels of all descriptions participated in the disastrous operation. Under German pressure, cargo loading was haphazard and discipline almost nonexistent. *Luftflotte 1* bombers preyed on the 15-mile-long convoy, sinking 18 ships; 13 transports and 18 warships fell victim to mines while Finnish torpedo boats accounted for even more. Ultimately only one transport reached Kronshtadt 200 miles away and the Germans pulled 12,000 soldiers out of the sea, while a further 10,000 perished.

* * *

After considerable success during Barbarossa's first two weeks, when it advanced 270 miles, Army Group North required an entire month to advance just 75 miles. Hitler complained openly to Halder about von Leeb's failures, while the Army Group's success carried it into inhospitable terrain and stiffening enemy resistance.

Failure to concentrate Fourth Panzer Group deprived it of much of its punch. The talents of General Reinhardt, "one of the best Panzer leaders" according to von Lossberg, were poorly utilized. As the gap between Army Group North's right and Army Group Center's left increased, so did the danger to both. Although David Glantz considers the Soltsy counterattack a failure, in reality it prompted a German overreaction.

At the highest levels German command suffered a meltdown. The normally persuasive Hitler wanted to keep pressure on Leningrad but

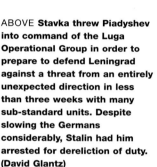

ABOVE **Stavka threw Piadyshev into command of the Luga Operational Group in order to prepare to defend Leningrad against a threat from an entirely unexpected direction in less than three weeks with many sub-standard units. Despite slowing the Germans considerably, Stalin had him arrested for dereliction of duty. (David Glantz)**

TOP, RIGHT **Soviet partisans were especially active in the north and particularly effective in the broken, wooded, and swampy terrain that the Germans encountered as they pressed further into Russia. Here some mine a road while their comrades keep watch for German troops. (US National Archives)**

BOTTOM, RIGHT **Generals Busch, von Richthofen, and Wiktorin (XXVIII Army Corps) plan an assault on the Luga River defenses. The entire nature of Barbarossa's northern theater changed at this point, when the Soviets' cobbled-together defenses, terrain, and weather conspired to halt the Germans only a few days' march from Leningrad. (Podzun Verlag)**

could not impose his will on senior generals beguiled by Moscow. Logistics hamstrung Army Group North as well; fuel consumption was three times the pre-Barbarossa estimates. By mid-summer von Leeb had ten of the *Ostheer's* "stricken" divisions, while Luftwaffe maintenance officers went in search of wrecked aircraft to scavenge for repair parts.

On the Soviet side, Kuznetsov had failed to manage a coherent defense anywhere. Therefore the Germans threatened Leningrad from unexpected directions, south and southeast. Three days into Barbarossa, General Popov noted the advantages of defending his city along the Luga River. Increasingly Soviet defensive efforts centered on *ad hoc* formations such as the LOG. Superfluous echelons of command, such as corps, were eliminated just to add another, the Direction. Reorganized units commonly lost attached formations; infantry units were stripped of tank, anti-tank, and anti-aircraft elements, which in turn became stand-alone entities.

A Gefreiter chalks up another "kill" on the radio sponson of an early model Sturmgeschütz III. The assault gun commander, an Oberleutnant wearing the field-gray panzer jacket of the Sturmartillerie, leans out of his hatch. (US National Archives)

Popov was a highly regarded general commanding the prestigious Leningrad Military District. He served as operational commander at Leningrad under the figurehead Voroshilov until Zhukov's arrival. (David Glantz)

Less than two months into Barbarossa most of the prewar Red Army had ceased to exist. Its entire first echelon had vanished trying to implement DP 41. However, while the Red Army foundered, the Soviet state reacted decisively. It immediately mobilized new forces, evacuated significant portions of its economy and industry beyond the Nazis' reach and Stalin reorganized the national leadership for a war of attrition. Now a new, but predictable, threat emerged from another direction: Finland.

# FINLAND AND THE ARCTIC

Germany abandoned its early neutrality in the Russo-Finnish conflict, and by August 1940 stationed technical troops in Finland, mainly to improve railroads and airfields. During his visit to Berlin in November, Molotov not only refused Hitler's bait that the USSR redirect its ambitions away from Europe and toward southwest Asia, he also asked Germany to remove its troops from Finland. Hitler's indirect answer was to tell Wehrmacht leaders on 5 December to count on Finnish participation in Barbarossa.

Axis forces in the far north had three missions: to protect Norway, to secure the nickel mines at Petsamo, and to cut the Murmansk railroad. Finland would "… tie down the maximum Russian forces by an attack west of, or on both sides of, Lake Ladoga …" By 27 January von Falkenhorst's staff planned Operation *Silberfuchs*. This overambitious plan envisioned a German assault toward Salla from central Finland to cut the rail line followed by a turn north to capture Murmansk. The Finns would attack toward Ladoga and the Svir River.

After the Royal Navy raid against the Norwegian coast on 4 March, Hitler over-reacted in a manner sure to cripple Barbarossa's chances in the north; he assigned 160 artillery batteries to Norway's defense and prohibited most of the 150,000 troops in Norway from participating in Barbarossa.

That spring General Dietl flew to Berlin to appeal to Hitler. The Führer called the 60 miles from Norway to Murmansk "laughable." Dietl stressed the bare rocks, lack of vegetation, and the swampy permafrost. Logistics would be a nightmare; most supplies would have to go by sea to Narvik then along the unreliable 300-mile *Reichstrasse 50* (most Finnish ports were too small and ice-bound for four to five months). He argued against attempting to both capture the port and cut the rail line. After all, if they cut the railroad, then Murmansk would be worthless. Hitler would not hear of it; von Falkenhorst would have to proceed with both attacks.

For its part, Finland was primarily interested in liberating its lost Karelian lands. Many senior Finnish officers had served in the 27th Prussian Jägers during the Great War and so had some familiarity with the German military, but were cautious in dealing with the Wehrmacht. Their Chief of Staff, General Heinrichs visited Jodl from 25–27 May 1941. The German explained that a costly siege of Leningrad would be unnecessary due to the expected speedy Soviet disintegration.

Command and control represented the weakest link in Fenno-German arrangements. Hitler made von Falkenhorst's main goal the defense of Norway. Hitler considered the general "unlucky" despite German success during the 1940 Scandinavian campaign. He wanted

A hasty divisional officers' conference takes place surrounded by a variety of vehicles (clockwise from top): an SdKfz 251 half-track, SdKfz 263 eight-wheel command vehicle, a Horsch Pkw staff car, motorcycle, and Flak gun mounted on a Krupp L2H143 "Schnauzer." (History in the Making)

Mannerheim to command all Axis forces in the far north. The marshal refused, knowing in that case Finland would have no military or political freedom of action. Unity of command and effort would be a mirage in Finland, and indeed along Barbarossa's entire northern flank.

### Operation *Platinfuchs*

On *Barbarossatag* von Falkenhorst ordered the Mountain Corps Norway to attack in one week. Dietl had 27,500 men in two divisions plus an engineer and signal battalion, half a Flak battalion, a panzer company, and a *Nebelwerfer* battery. Preparatory to the general assault the 2nd Mountain Division moved from Kirkenes to Petsamo and the 3rd marched from Narvik to Loustari. Colonel Andreas Nielsen, who had been present at Hitler's 1923 Beer Hall Putsch in Munich, led Luftwaffe forces consisting of 36 Stukas, 11 Ju-52s, ten bombers, and ten fighters. Dietl's mission was to attack to Motovka on the Litsa River and then press on to Murmansk. He placed the 2nd Mountain Division, which was to constitute the *Schwerpunkt*, on the left, and 3rd Mountain Division on the right. His armored reserve, 1/Panzer Battalion 40, waited at Petsamo. The Soviets defended with their 14th Rifle Division forward while the 52nd Rifle moved up from near Murmansk.

The assault began as planned on the 29th, and with panzer support a *Kampfgruppe* of the 3rd Mountain reached the Titovka River the next day. At that point roads shown on German maps ceased to exist. Dietl therefore pulled the 3rd out of the line and placed it behind the 2nd. Events had derailed his plans in less than 24 hours, and within a week Northern Fleet warships landed Red Army soldiers behind German lines. Between 7 and 8 July, Dietl's men crossed the Litsa River but Soviet counterattacks pushed them back.

Dietl developed a less ambitious plan that took account of terrain and logistics difficulties. He attacked the 205th Rifle Regiment on 12 July, had seven battalions across the Litsa the next day but the Soviet Navy landed 1,350 soldiers behind his lines on 14 July. Up to that point the small *Jäger* divisions had used one regiment to fight and the other to run supplies forward on mule trains. Increasingly, however, combat forces accumulated in the bridgeheads and logistics ground to a halt.

A week later von Falkenhorst and Dietl met and attempted, unsuccessfully, to persuade Hitler to release three regiments of the Norwegian garrison. On 24 July they decided it would be futile to continue the offensive unless they received reinforcements within one month. At the end of July Hitler relented, promising Schörner's 6th Mountain Division by the second half of September. Prompted by Royal Navy attacks against Kirkenes and Petsamo, on 12 August the Führer also agreed to transfer the 9th SS and 388th Infantry Regiments from Norway.

With Allied ships outnumbering its five destroyers, two U-boats, and various smaller vessels, the Kriegsmarine was losing the battle at sea. Rear Admiral A.G. Golovko's Northern Fleet mustered a cruiser, eight destroyers, three large and eight small torpedo boats, 27 submarines and 45 other craft. Just as Dietl prepared to resume his attack Soviet submarines sank two German merchantmen full of reinforcements. On 8 September the Royal Navy chased other cargo ships into Norwegian fjords. British naval pressure delayed the 6th Mountain Division for weeks.

The Germans suffered from a similar disadvantage in the air. Major General A. Kuznetsov commanded combined Red Air Force and naval air elements in the north. His 49 bombers, 139 fighters, and 44 floatplanes more than held their own against Nielsen's force.

After constant delays, Jodl visited Mountain Corps headquarters to investigate difficulties there. On 5 September Dietl told him Murmansk was out of the question even with the 6th Mountain's help. Both agreed Schörner's men would only further stress the logistics chain. In addition, the Soviets had by now reinforced their lines; the 14th and 52nd Rifle Divisions stood north and south of the Ura Gubo road, and the "Polyarnyy" (Polar) Militia Division held the left flank.

Nevertheless Dietl attacked on 8 September and made good initial progress. In the 2nd Mountain's southern sector, the inexperienced 388th Infantry Regiment bypassed part of the 14th Rifle Division, which promptly counterattacked into the *Landsers'* rear. The same happened further north shortly thereafter to the untried 9th SS Regiment. Dietl suspended operations for 24 hours to stabilize the situation and bring up supplies. The 3rd Mountain struggled forward until 16 September. Dietl cancelled the assault on 21 September and ordered his men to occupy good defensive positions.

The 6th Mountain arrived from Greece to relieve the 2nd and 3rd by mid-October. In two and a half months Dietl advanced 22 miles at a cost of 10,000 casualties with over 30 miles left to go. Terrain favored the defenders and Red Army supplies only had to travel 40–50 miles from Murmansk. For the mountain corps Barbarossa's road to Murmansk had been anything but "laughable."

## Operation *Polarfuchs*

General Feige commanded the scaled-down attack toward Kandalaksha and the Soviet rail line. His XXXVI Corps consisted of the 169th Infantry Division, 6th "Nord" (minus the 9th Regiment), two panzer, two motorized artillery, and two engineer battalions, half a Flak battalion and a *Nebelwerfer* battery, totaling over 40,000 men. Its mission was to attack along the road from Rovaniemi to Kandalaksha, and later turn north to

*Gebirgsjäger* on outpost duty near the Arctic Circle. What the Lapland theater lacked in mountainous altitude it made up in northern latitude. Dietl, in common with von Leeb, also fought a "poor man's war" in the far north. (History in the Making)

link up with Dietl. The Finnish III Corps, basically their 6th Division, added a supporting attack to Allakurtti. The Luftwaffe contributed 30 Stukas and ten bombers, ten fighters, and ten reconnaissance planes. German intelligence identified the Soviet defenders as the 122nd Rifle Division supported by approximately 50 tanks.

The Axis plan called for the 169th Infantry to encircle Salla with two thirds of its strength while the remaining regiment made a frontal assault on the Red Army defenses. The two regiments of "Nord" would also attack south of Salla. With nearly 24 hours of daylight, the Germans attacked at "night" on 1 July with the sun to their backs.

"Nord" encountered stubborn resistance and very heavy defensive fire. On 2 July the attack was called off. "Nord" spent two days preparing to resume the attack but early on 4 July the Soviets launched a counterattack of their own. Although the attack was beaten back by army and Finnish units, troops streamed to the rear with tales of a breakthrough by Soviet tanks, demanding all bridges blown up behind them. "Nord" had been organized for police duty in Norway but nevertheless their poor conduct infuriated Hitler, who ordered the division back to the front. Luckily the Red Army was unable to exploit these failings.

Two days later Feige reorganized and attacked again. Armored support consisted of Panzer Battalion 40 (less the company with Dietl) and Panzer Battalion 211 (equipped with captured Hotchkiss and Somua tanks). Armor was restricted to traveling on main roads (minor roads were too poor) so those panzers actually in combat seldom amounted to more than two companies. With artillery support and close air support, five battalions of the 169th and the panzers advanced and attacked the town. The 122nd Rifle evacuated Salla, leaving behind 50 tanks. The next day "Nord," the only motorized unit in the Army of Norway, took up the pursuit. The 122nd fell back through the 104th Rifle Division to refit.

General Feige sought to create a *Kessel* east of Apa Lakes with the XXXVI Corps, reinforced by Infantry Regiment 324, advancing around from the north and the Finnish 6th Division and Panzer Battalion 211 from the south. Major General H. Siilasvou's Finnish III Corps made good

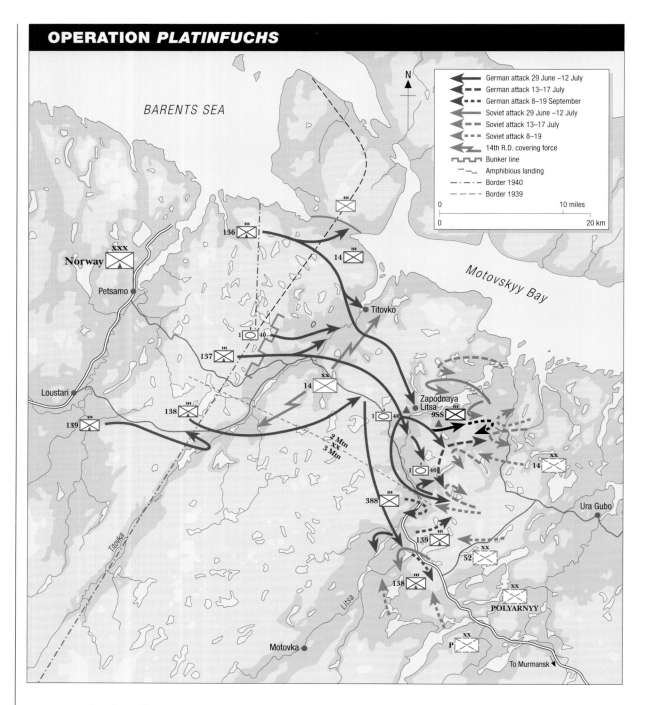

progress using "*motti*" tactics (quick, small encirclements – rather than the larger ones favored by the Germans). At this point, 22 August, the 169th Infantry and remainder of "Nord" broke free northeast of Salla, trapping the 104th and 122nd Rifle Divisions, who eventually fell back. The cordon in the German sector was especially porous and weather prevented a Luftwaffe "vertical envelopment," with the result that the Red Army troops managed to escape the trap, albeit without their heavy equipment. The 6th Finnish and 169th Infantry Divisions pursued to Allakurtti without the

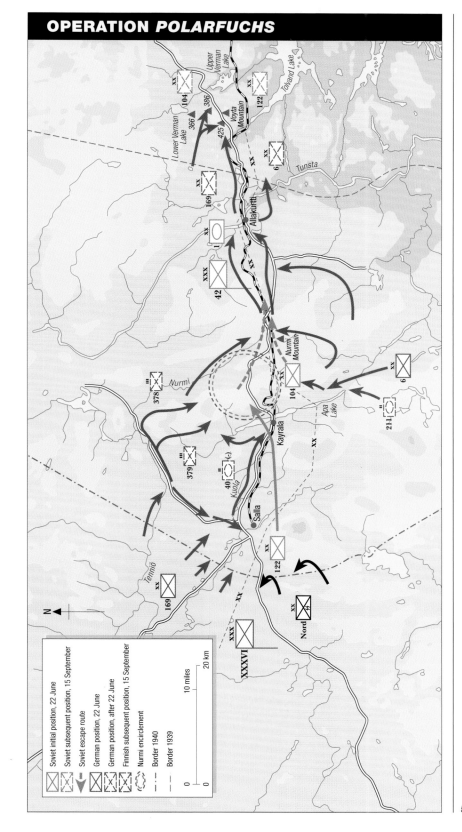

panzers, which were too heavy for the terrain and bridges in the area. The town was taken from the north on 1 September. Remnants of the 104th and 122nd Rifle Divisions deployed along the Voytayoki River line, and eventually fell back along the Vermanyoki River. The front stabilized.

At the southern edge of the German area, slow German preparations gave the Soviets time to reinforce, angering von Falkenhorst. From 16–23 July he badgered Feige at the latter's headquarters until the XXXVI Corps committed to attack down the Kasten'ga axis on 26 July. The terrain rendered the panzers practically useless, and with the Luftwaffe elements commanded from Oslo, their close air support was ineffective. As the *Schwerpunkt* shifted north and south the panzers marched and countermarched, engineers cutting new roads each time. Meanwhile, the Finns continued their advance augmented by elements of "Nord," most of Panzer Battalion 40, and Stuka close air support, arriving at Kasten'ga on 7 August. The Soviets raced their 88th Rifle over from Belomorsk. By mid-month Group "J" (six battalions) and three battalions of "Nord" were exhausted. The Finns switched their main effort to Group "F," which attacked in the rain on 19 August completely surprising the defenders.

Führer Directive 36 of 22 September ordered resumption of the Kandalaksha offensive. Delays hampered Feige until Führer Directive 37 (10 October) cancelled further attacks, stating that the Soviet position along the main front appeared to be on the point of imminent collapse. Hitler halted the assault just when the situation began to look bright and the Soviets were at the end of their endurance. Group "F" advanced until 15 November. Five days later, about 40 miles from the railroad, both sides halted and sought good defensive terrain.

## Karelia

By the summer of 1941 Finland had mobilized 16 divisions, two brigades of *Jägers* (light troops mounted on bicycles in summer), and one cavalry brigade totaling 450,000 men. It possessed experienced leaders and troops, restocked supplies, new German automatic weapons plus 105mm and 120mm artillery. It had seven platoons of British and captured Soviet tanks, and 152 aircraft in its air force. However Finland's war was not Germany's war. Finnish strategy was mainly to secure easily defended lines across Karelia and along the Svir River. As good "brothers in arms," the Finns would neutralize the Soviet base at Hanko and assist Army Group North by threatening Leningrad. Significantly, Mannerheim had few illusions about leaving behind the relative security of the Finnish forests and venturing too far into the more open Russian terrain.

Finnish forces in Karelia accounted for over half her military manpower – 230,000 men, compared to the Soviets 150,000 men. Karelia was defended by General Gerasimov's 23rd Army with four rifle divisions, and Meretskov's 7th Independent Army with five rifle divisions. At Hanko the Finnish 17th Division faced two rifle brigades and 23,000 Soviets. Two Finnish divisions and the German 163rd Infantry Division (less the 388th Regiment) represented Mannerheim's reserve.

**Phase I:** After the requisite provocation following *Barbarossatag* of Soviet air raids and a tank attack, General Heinrich's Army of Karelia north of Lake Ladoga moved out on 10 July. Attacking north of Lake Yanis on the Finnish

A group of casual-looking Finnish soldiers. The Finns bested the Red Army every time the two clashed, but Finland's limited objectives minimized its contributions to Hitler's crusade in the east. (History in the Making)

left, VI Corps and Group "O" created a breakthrough at Kopisel'kaya. The 71st Rifle Division gave way and the Jägers occupied Muanto on 14 July, followed by Koirinoye on Ladoga's north coast on the 16th. The Finns had covered 65 miles in ten days and trapped much of the 7th Army between the frontier and Lake Ladoga. VI and VII Corps applied frontal pressure, reaching the Yanis River on 17 July against ineffective Soviet resistance. Finnish 1st and German 163rd Infantry Divisions covered the far left flank.

VI Corps took Salmi on 21 July, following a three-day battle. On the 24th, Red Army counterattacks forced the Finns to assume a defensive posture. The understrength 163rd Infantry Division, now alone in the north, became bogged down. A VI Corps' attack toward Suvilakhti failed to rectify the situation. VII Corps exerted pressure on the 168th Rifle Division barely hanging on in Sortavala by the end of July. The Finns, now under command of I Corps, continued to push forward. However, weak Luftwaffe and Finnish Air Force elements precluded an effective vertical envelopment, and these Soviets showed no more willingness to surrender than those encircled elsewhere during Barbarossa. Late in August the Ladoga Flotilla evacuated the bulk of the 142nd, 168th, and 198th Rifle Divisions across the lake.

On 31 August, II Corps began its assault south of Lake Ladoga. By 5 August, Mannerheim, in direct control of the northern elements, moved up his reserve 10th Division. Keksgol'm fell the same day and in combination these maneuvers cut off two more Red Army divisions.

On 13 August Mannerheim ordered II Corps south toward Pakkola on the Vuosalmi River. The 18th Division won a bridgehead there on the 18th. This move threatened the Vyborg fortress from the east. IV Corps began the frontal assault on 22 August. Three days later the 8th Division crossed the bay, cut the rail line to Primorsk and completed the encirclement of Vyborg, trapping three rifle divisions. A Soviet counterattack opened a hole long enough for the 43rd and 123rd Rifle Divisions to escape. IV Corps troops entered the fortress on the 29th. Leaving their equipment and vehicles behind, a third rifle division retreated first to Koivisto Island then, in late-November, to Leningrad. With IV Corps pressing on the right and I Corps (again reassigned a new sector) on the left, the Soviet 23rd Army withdrew behind the 1939 border by the end of August. Outside Leningrad the front stabilized barely five miles south of the old frontier for the next three years.

Unresolved issues began to bedevil Fenno-German strategy; a binding agreement never existed between the two nations. Two months into Barbarossa, Keitel wrote a letter to Mannerheim asking the Finns to attack past the Svir in order to link up with von Leeb. The marshal showed the letter to President Risto Ryti; both men agreed advancing beyond the Svir was not in Finland's interests and that "under no circumstances" would they attack Leningrad, clearly "a German task." The Finns feared that Army Group North would get no further than Volkhov and that Finland would have to push further forward to effect a juncture.

**Phase II:** On 4 September Jodl arrived at Mannerheim's Mikkeli headquarters with Iron- and Knight's Cross decorations for the marshal. Following their largest artillery preparation of the war the Finns began a general offensive that same day. VI Corps shoved aside the 3rd Rifle Division and reached the Svir in three days. Elements of the 17th Division captured the Svir Station the next day, cutting the Murmansk railroad.

T-34 tanks negotiate a ravine in Karelia. A stillborn attack two miles into Finland by elements of the 21st Tank Division on 2 July provided the "provocation" Finland needed to the attack the USSR. (History in the Making)

Until reinforcements arrived, the Siberian 114th Rifle Division held the river line against all threats. VII Corps made slower progress toward Lake Onega, finally capturing Petrozavodsk on 1 October after a two-week fight. At this point many Finns considered "their" war won, so morale and discipline began to wane.

After regrouping, II Corps and Group "O" attacked north toward the upper Svir and the Stalin Canal on 19 October. Passing west and east of Lake Lizhm, the two pincers joined on 5 November. One month later the Finns reached Medvezh'yegorsk, destroyed two rifle divisions, cut the Murmansk rail connection again, and went onto the defensive on 6 December. Three days earlier the Soviets evacuated Hanko under virtually no Finnish pressure.

\* \* \*

Axis operations in the far north failed for a number of reasons, primarily few common interests and disjointed command and control. The Germans were neither equipped, trained, nor inclined to fight effectively in the theater. They consistently underestimated the Red Army's strength in terrain that particularly favored the defender. The Soviets also had the flexibility to transfer forces laterally along the Murmansk railroad. Likewise Luftwaffe air support lacked its usual effectiveness: it was too weak for the massive frontage; it shifted *Schwerpunkt* constantly with changing objectives and weather often grounded its missions.

The importance of Archangel and Murmansk as supply conduits was obvious from the Great War. Nevertheless the far north represented Barbarossa's poor relation. The Finns cut the Karelia rail line twice, but an eastern line ran uninterrupted. The Luftwaffe breached this eastern rail line over 100 times in 1941 alone but the Soviets quickly repaired the roadbed. Ju-88 pilots claimed that due to anti-aircraft fire they would "rather fly over London three times than once over Murmansk." Although potentially of great importance, the theater became a backwater of Barbarossa.

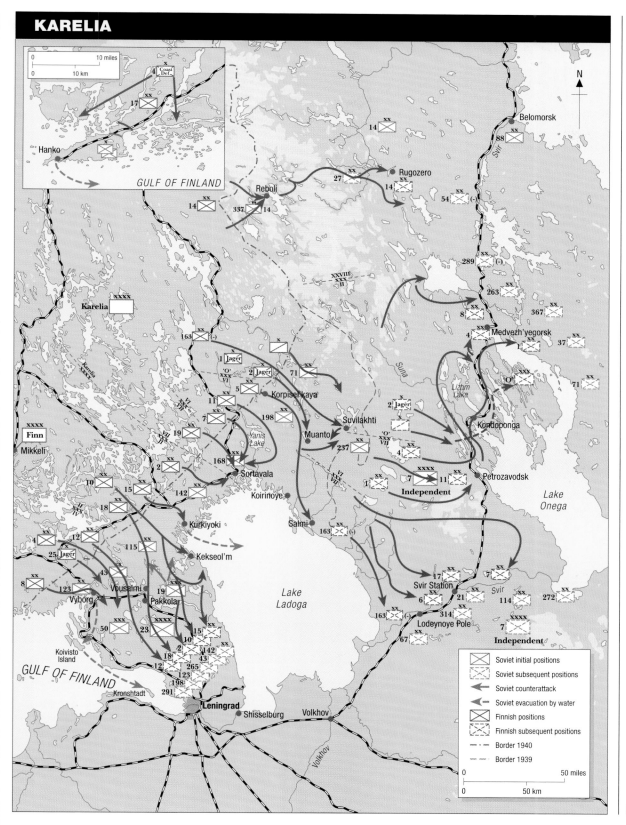

# CLOSING ON LENINGRAD

Meanwhile, von Leeb's panzers continued to diverge like fingers on an open hand. To compound matters the results of the Finns' attack across Karelia were the opposite of what the Germans had hoped for. The high command had too much hope of linking up on the Svir River and therefore placed more emphasis on von Manstein's right hook than was justified. Lacking mass, each panzer corps fought in near isolation over terrain that favored the defenders while the infantry armies were likewise dangerously dispersed.

Now Hitler and his generals began arguing in earnest over Barbarossa's future. Other factors impacted on von Leeb's plans. On the Army Group's right, supply problems delayed the Sixteenth Army's attack five times between 22 July and 6 August. Weather repeatedly grounded Luftwaffe air support, further postponing planned attacks across the front from Tallinn to Lake Il'men. On 7 August, von Leeb's meteorological staff told him the weather next day would be good.

Finally at 0900hrs on 8 August the general offensive began along the Luga River. Advances were limited to two–three miles that day. Hoepner reinforced XLI Panzer Corps with the 8th Panzer and 36th Motorized Divisions and slowly Reinhardt pried the defenders out. Von Manstein attacked at Luga on the 10th, also making halting progress against the 41st Rifle Corps. Hoepner changed his *Schwerpunkt* back and forth between his two panzer corps in order to gain some advantage. In four days XLI Panzer suffered 1,600 casualties and LVI Panzer 900.

Reinhardt finally achieved a hard-won breakthrough on 12–13 August. The next day 8th Panzer swung south in order to meet von Manstein's men coming up from the town of Luga. But first Vatutin

**Artillerymen of the 212th Infantry Division ride on a caisson as they approach Utorgosh west of Lake Il'men. For them the war of movement would soon be over as they now had to fight through successive defensive lines guarding Leningrad. (US National Archives)**

launched a counterattack to relieve pressure on Leningrad's defenders. This attack and the German reaction had a significant impact on the final assault.

**German Command Crisis and Final Drive**

On 21 July Hitler, Keitel, two staff officers, some SS bodyguards, and propaganda photographers arrived by air at Army Group North headquarters. Hitler appeared "pale and nervous." His only visit to von Leeb during Barbarossa accomplished nothing substantial. None of the participants knew it then, but the German high command was in the middle of a five-week debate over strategic decisions on the campaign's future during the prime summer campaigning season.

Not satisfied with his own visit, Hitler sent Paulus, considered an expert in mechanized warfare, to Army Group North headquarters on 24 and 26 July. Instead of convincing Hoepner to continue attacking between Lakes Peipus and Il'men (i.e., with LVI Panzer) he returned to the *Wolfschanze* reporting the area was completely unsuited for panzers. Hitler sent Keitel back north on 30 July with the promised assistance of *VIII Fliegerkorps.* Von Leeb told him the Army Group needed 35 divisions but had only 26, and that the Sixteenth Army could not adequately defend its 200-mile-plus front.

The Germans' self-inflicted command paralysis of late July and much of August is arguably the most critical non-structural factor in Barbarossa's failure. Following a month of stunning initial victories Germany's highest leadership figuratively shut down while Hitler worked through personal illness to impose his will on fractious and obstinate generals.

On 19 and 23 July Hitler issued his Directive 33 plus a Supplement that essentially ordered Third Panzer Group north from the Moscow axis toward Leningrad, leaving Moscow to Army Group Center's infantry. The supplement went so far as to subordinate Third Panzer Group to von Leeb. It correctly implied that two panzer groups would give the final push on Leningrad greater freedom of maneuver. Clearly Army Group North was not strong enough to accomplish its assigned missions alone. Hoth's six divisions would assist Hoepner to encircle Red Army forces in the north and prevent Soviet reinforcement and resupply of the Leningrad area. But Soviet resistance around the Smolensk pocket took longer than expected to reduce, delaying Hoth's departure. In these orders Hitler re-established capturing Leningrad as a pre-requisite for turning on Moscow as discussed at his conference on 5 December. However, this went against Halder's fixation on Moscow.

These orders confused, more than clarified, Barbarossa's objectives and future. Therefore Hitler issued Directive 34 on 30 July, also followed by a Supplement, on 12 August. In them he reasserted the primacy of Leningrad, specifically pushing von Leeb to swing wide right and link up with the Finns. Directive 34 further delayed any assistance from Army Group Center and sent Hoth's men only so far as the Valdai Heights. Hitler stressed encircling Leningrad by linking up with the Finnish Army. The supplement spoke of the need to "relieve Army Group North of anxiety about its right flank." Most significantly it stated that before attacking Moscow "operations against Leningrad must be concluded." The Führer still acceded to Army Group Center's desire to retain most of

## 269TH INFANTRY DIVISION SOLDIERS USING CAPTURED ANTI-TANK GUNS TO DESTROY SOVIET T-34 TANKS, JULY 1941 (pages 60–61)

The USSR dominated tank design during the interwar years; chief among their innovative weapons was the T-34. Although Stalin's purges delayed its development, T-34s were available in large numbers by *Barbarossatag*. A similar but heavier tank using the same gun was the KV-1 and its infantry-support variant, the KV-2. German military intelligence knew of these weapons in late-1940, but word was slow getting out to forces in the field. Most German unit histories mark their outfit's first encounter with these tanks as a very significant event. Four days into Barbarossa, German Army experts showed Hitler the new tank models at his East Prussian headquarters. Common German anti-tank weapons failed miserably against the new Soviet armor. Guns on panzers and in anti-tank battalions were inadequate. It was not unusual for Soviet tanks to receive many dozens and even hundreds of hits with no appreciable effect. A lucky shot might hit a vulnerable spot such as its optics, the turret ring or part of its suspension could occasionally knock out a tank. Otherwise panzermen tried to work their way to the back of one of the tanks and shoot it in the lightly armored rear. Therefore by necessity German tactics depended on the Red Army's poor driving techniques, non-existent maintenance, or inability to resupply its armor with fuel or ammunition. Then the massive and otherwise invulnerable tank might be driven into a marsh, break down, or coast to a stop with its fuel tanks empty. Often only in such a helpless condition could the Germans defeat Soviet armor. However, as the *Ostheer* advanced it captured thousands of pieces of Red Army hardware either thrown down by retreating defenders or rounded up in huge encirclements. It also captured massive quantities of Soviet ammunition in supply depots. The ZiS-3 76mm anti-tank gun (1) was a modification of a standard field gun of the same size. Like the T-34 and Il-2 Sturmovik airplane, the ZiS-3 is recognized as one of the premier weapons of World War II. As another field-expedient method of destroying Soviet armor, the Germans became adept at turning these fine weapons against their former owners within minutes of capturing them. German anti-tank gunners quickly discarded their own equipment and turned captured Red Army pieces 180°. Members of the 269th Infantry Division are shown here attempting to keep up with Reinhardt's XLI Panzer Corps as it advances across the marshy terrain between the Velikaya and Luga Rivers. The *Landsers* occupy temporary defensive positions but as soon as they dig out a spadeful of dirt the hole fills with brackish water (2). The German anti-tank gun crew prepares to put the piece into operation (3). A couple of infantry squads provide security to the flanks (4). Suddenly they hear the distinctive rumble of a tank engine, accompanied by the chirping of metal on metal and tracks on sprockets. Across the marshy meadow the T-34 comes out of the tree line on a forest trail (5). A shot, a hit, but not the kill they wanted. They reload for another try as the buttoned-up turret scans to determine where the danger came from. (Peter Dennis)

**Panzer troops interrogate a Soviet POW. The officer with his back to the camera wears a black panzer jacket while the German tank crewman center wears the mouse-gray "Trikot" shirt. The odds that the Red Army prisoner survived German captivity are very slim. (US National Archives)**

Hoth's Panzer Group. The supplement confirmed the earlier Leningrad–Moscow timing. However, the Soviets still had an influence on events and soon caused great trouble exactly where the Germans feared it most – on Busch's "anxious" flank.

Needless to say, Halder was disgusted with all four documents but by the end of August he held the losing hand and Hitler demanded Leningrad be taken as soon as possible. Von Manstein later wrote that "the open tug-of-war between Hitler and OKH over further operational goals [Moscow or Leningrad] prevailed" over the need to cooperate in order to insure Barbarossa's success. Halder used Hitler's illness, von Brauchitsch, Jodl, and even Guderian to thwart the dictator. For his part, the army commander was too tired either to support Halder or fight Hitler. Von Lossberg commented that after the summer leadership crisis "it was only a matter of time until von Brauchitsch was relieved."

As happened elsewhere along Barbarossa's front during this high-level tomfoolery, operational commanders took matters into their own hands. Intrigue at the strategic level did not equal inactivity at the operational or tactical levels. With the LVI Panzer Corps bogged down on the road to Novgorod, on 15 July Hoepner decided Reinhardt would attack Leningrad alone. Von Leeb visited the panzer group command post the next day, approved this decision and returned I Army Corps to Hoepner as flank protection. By late July LXI Panzer waited for von Manstein who spent six weeks trying to negotiate the Luga Line. On 30 July a frustrated Reinhardt again wrote in his diary, "More delays. It's terrible. The chance we opened up [to Leningrad] has been lost for good…" Defending the Sabsk bridgeheads cost more casualties than attacking.

Meanwhile the Kremlin was having its own command and control problems. Relying on leadership by fear, commissars "advised" with threats though most commanders did everything possible under the circumstances.

The situation improved slightly under Voroshilov, but as the Germans approached Leningrad the old marshal created the Military Soviet for the Defense of Leningrad, probably to spread the blame for anticipated failures. During the second half of August, Stalin dispatched a deputation

A Stuka flies over the bombed-out ruins of Novgorod the day after a massive *VIII Fliegerkorps* attack. The walled Kremlin and Volkhov River (lower left) are clearly visible. (US National Archives)

from his own headquarters to rectify the situation. His men broke up the *ad hoc* Soviet and dismissed the entire leadership of the Northwest Front (Voroshilov received a temporary face-saving position as Leningrad Commander) until Zhukov arrived on 9 September.

### Sixteenth Army: Staraya Russa and Demyansk

Meanwhile Vatutin husbanded remnants of the 11th and 27th Armies plus the new 34th and 48th Armies to attack Army Group North's extended eastern flank. He originally created over-optimistic plans of striking Busch on both sides of Lake Il'men and advancing ten miles per day. Stavka told him this was "clearly beyond the capacity" of the front and instructed him to settle on a more "limited mission." Vatutin therefore decided to attack south of the lake on 3 or 4 August and try for two–three miles per day. The attack was delayed, first by the writing of new orders and poor weather, then by the Germans' Luga offensive, until 12 August. On the flanks, the 48th Army aimed for Novgorod while the 27th moved on Kholm. In the center, supported by the 11th Army, the robust 34th Army represented the main effort, driving into the 30-mile gap between the Sixteenth Army's X and II Corps.

German intelligence failed to spot Soviet preparations. The 27th Army did not make much progress against Kholm but the 34th advanced 24 miles to cut the Dno–Staraya Russa railroad by 14 August. Hansen's three divisions fell back in front of Major General K.M. Kachalov's 12 divisions. Soon the same miserable terrain with which Army Group North had to contend, plus poor command and control, conspired to slow the offensive. Dno represented Busch's headquarters and a logistics hub supporting much of the Leningrad offensive. The gap between the two corps grew to almost 50 miles as Vatutin added four divisions to his order of battle. The German 30th Infantry Division abandoned Staraya Russa on 16 August. A 30-mile retreat, following their strenuous advance and defensive battle, further exhausted the *Landsers*. Von Leeb, and to a lesser degree Hitler, overestimated the impact of the Red Army attack. Halder called them "irrelevant pinpricks." Hoepner advocated keeping pressure on the lower Luga Line and even pulled LVI Panzer Corps out of the middle of Luga to reinforce Reinhardt for a final push on Leningrad.

However von Leeb refused to accept the risk of a weakened right, and transferred the 3rd Motorized and "Totenkopf" (plus *I Fliegerkorps* and *VIII Fliegerkorps* air support) from the Luga Line to Dno to prepare for a German counterattack. Under cover of the night von Manstein's divisions made a 150-mile march to reinforce a situation that was already stabilizing. On 19 August, first "Totenkopf" at 0300hrs and then 3rd Motorized Division unexpectedly struck the 34th Army like a hammer. Rain and Soviet resistance made the going rough. By 23 August the Germans restored the Lovat line, taking 18,000 POWs, 300 guns, 200 tanks, and the first *Katyusha* rocket launchers to fall into their hands. The bulk of four rifle divisions and one cavalry division were crushed.

Ironically, about the same time as LVI Panzer Corps regained the line of the Lovat River, General of Panzer Troops Adolf Kuntzen's LVII Panzer Corps[3] arrived. To reach that point, LVII Panzer began an attack at 0330hrs on 23 August toward Velikie Luki, following a bombardment by artillery,

**3** 19th and 20th Panzer Divisions plus two infantry regiments

*Nebelwerfer,* and Stuka dive-bombers. The nature of the terrain meant that the two panzer divisions operated almost independently. The battle for Velikie Luki ended on the 26th with another *Kessel* of 30,000 POWs. Although German losses were significant, Soviet dead lay in heaps. The bulk of the 22nd Army – 126th, 110th, 124th, 179th, 186th, 14th Rifle Divisions plus the 48th Tank Division – was destroyed. Kuntzen's men struggled northward while Red Army defenders made effective use of mines, anti-tank ditches, and fortified houses. The LVII Panzer Corps arrived at Kholm and linked up with Army Group North on 9 September.

Now united, the II and X Army Corps, plus the LVI and LVII Panzer Corps, headed east for Demyansk and the Valdai Hills beginning on 12 September. The flat, swampy ground, mud 18in. deep and undergrowth-clogged wilderness slowed the Germans. Moving at night for better concealment attracted partisans and cavalry. They reached Demyansk four days later in piecemeal fashion, but halted due to the desperate logistics situation. Ju-52 transport aircraft provided emergency resupply. By 18 September, however, most of the mobile formations were loading onto trains for the Moscow Front. The Sixteenth Army *Landsers* would henceforth be on their own.

Busch's men closed another small *Kessel* near the Valdai Heights, encircled 35,000 more Soviet troops, 334 guns, and 117 tanks. Finally the Sixteenth eliminated the "elusive" 11th and 27th Armies and the newer 34th Army. The 12th Infantry Division reached the source of the Volga near Lake Ostashkov (Seliger) in the Valdai Heights, essentially marking the end of Sixteenth Army's progress in Barbarossa.

Combined losses for the 11th, 27th, and 34th Armies from 10–31 August were 128,550 men (30 percent) and 481 tanks (89 percent), but von Leeb forfeited operational success on the critical Leningrad axis for tactical victory on a secondary front. Granted he secured the seam between the two army groups, but at a cost to the Germans in lost time and expended efforts that crippled the drive on Leningrad. Halder resisted reinforcing von Leeb with Hoth's Panzers for nearly a month only to relent by dispatching the XXXIX and LVII Panzer Corps northward when it was arguably too late for them to achieve more than limited success.

### The Eighteenth Army and the Baltic Islands

Lacking a third panzer corps with which to build a *Schwerpunkt,* Hoepner had to again wait for infantry to march forward to fulfill that role. Von Küchler's XXVI and XXXVIII Army Corps finally arrived on the Neva River in the second half of August. They had three missions: 1) shield the panzer group's left, 2) push the 8th Army north, and 3) destroy the 8th before it could add its strength to the defenses of Leningrad. These operations, plus Hoepner's final assault, would have to wait until the dramas around Staraya Russa and Demyansk played themselves out. Relegated to secondary front status, the Eighteenth Army's attention turned to the islands off the Estonian coast.

\* \* \*

In October 1917, Imperial Germany conducted Operation Albion, amphibious landings on the Baltic Islands. The *Nordkorps* landed on the seaward side, bagging 20,000 Russian POWs before moving on to Reval

A column of T-34s maneuver in the Novgorod sector. These tanks were superior to anything the Wehrmacht could field but German doctrine and crew skill cancelled any Soviet technical advantages. (History in the Making)

(Tallinn). A generation later von Leeb's men began planning Operation Beowulf on 29 April, originating on the Estonian mainland. Heavy fighting in the Eighteenth Army area, especially at Tallinn, plus the Kriegsmarine's difficulty in assembling amphibious craft repeatedly delayed "Beowulf." Soviet nuisance air raids launched from Saaremaa against Berlin between 7 August and 4 September gave the assault an added emphasis.

Saaremaa and Hiiumaa were the largest islands at approximately 1,000 and 500 square miles each. Smaller Muhu was connected to Saaremaa by a 2¼-mile-long causeway. All islands were flat, sandy, and rocky, covered with heather and generally inhabited by poor farmers and fishermen. Major General A.B. Elisseyev commanded 24,000 defenders (German intelligence identified 15,000) who had used the preceding ten weeks poorly and were ill-prepared. Initially two battalions of the 79th Rifle Regiment guarded Muhu while the 3rd Independent Rifle Brigade held Saaremaa. One Soviet strength was their ten coastal and 16 mobile artillery batteries.

The Germans wanted Elisseyev to think they were repeating their 1917 attack from the sea and thus on the night of 13 September the cruisers *Leipzig*, *Köln*, and *Emden* plus mine sweepers, sub-chasers, and torpedo boats conducted a feint to the west of the islands in Operation Südwind. In Operation Nordwind, the Finns did the same off the north shore of Hiiumaa with two monitors, two armed icebreakers, and various smaller vessels. Unfortunately for them their flagship, the 10in. gun monitor *Ilmarinen*, struck two mines and sank within seven minutes with a loss of 271 sailors. However, these naval ruses worked as the Soviets tried to defend the islands' coastline and were not ready when the real assault came.

"Beowulf's" plan called for the 61st Infantry Division to assault on 14 September, only 17 days after conquering Tallinn. The 151st, 162nd, and 176th Infantry Regiments would cross the six-mile sound to Muhu in turn, starting at 0400hrs. Brandenburger commandos parachuted in against coastal guns at Kuebassare (seaborne elements failed to arrive) and the Luftwaffe planned robust air support. The first wave in four–six man boats missed their intended beach by one mile as a result of strong winds and currents, as well as inexperienced crews. The second wave got so disoriented that they circled back to Estonia. *Aufklärungs Abteilung 161* landed on the north end of Muhu later in the day. By the first evening five infantry and one artillery (light mountain gun) battalions occupied a four-mile wide beachhead.

151st Infantry Regiment crossed the causeway against disorganized Soviet resistance on the 15 September; the defenders had not yet recovered from the deception plan. 151st and 162nd Infantry Regiments advanced down the southern side of Saaremaa while *Aufklärungs Abteilung 161* and the 176th Regiment moved along the north coast. Resupply came in the form of huge Bf 321 "Gigant" transport gliders. The capital Kuresaare fell on the 21st.

Soviet remnants numbering 15,000 retreated to the Sorve Peninsula for a final defense. Beginning on 23 September, first 162nd Infantry Regiment then 151st assaulted the 1½-mile wide isthmus. Fighting ended there on 5 October. Haenicke's men captured 5,000 POWs while many escaped to Hiiumaa. Throughout the operation I/KG77 and II/ZG26 provided invaluable air support, coordinated by the air-control ship *Karl Meyer* steaming in the Baltic.

*Landsers* of the 290th Infantry Division fighting in Staraya Russa during the second half of August; the town changed hands three times that month. (History in the Making)

Soviet engineers belonging to the 34th Army emplacing mines amongst anti-tank obstacles in August. At this point they were engaged in a seesaw battle against the Sixteenth Army south of Lake Il'men. (History in the Making)

Preceded by another naval feint and supported by gunfire from the *Köln* and other ships, the 176th Infantry Regiment landed on the east side of Hiiumaa at 0500hrs on 12 October in Operation Siegfried. Surprise was complete once again. *Aufklärungs Abteilung 161* and the 151st Regiment followed on the west and central axes. Severe terrain limited the effectiveness of motorized *Kampfgruppe Sierigk*. The battle for Hiiumaa lasted nine days against often stubborn resistance by 3,000–5,000 Soviets.

General Haenicke commanded another exemplary operation after receiving the Knight's Cross for his 61st Infantry Division's role in taking Tallinn weeks earlier. Aided by naval units, and Bf 110s as flying artillery, his men eliminated the threat of artillery interdiction of Riga Bay. At a cost of 2,850 casualties they captured 15,000 POWs, and over 200 guns. Poor Red Army leadership, specifically weak command and control, and ineffective use of reserves, handed the Germans a satisfying tactical victory.

# SOVIET ATTACKS AROUND STARAYA RUSSA, AUGUST 1941

Soviet attacks south of Staraya Russa and German counterattack,
12–23 August 1941. Viewed from the southeast shows General Vatutin's
attack to distract Army Group North and take pressure off Red Army defenders
in front of Leningrad.

Note: Gridlines are shown at intervals of 10 km

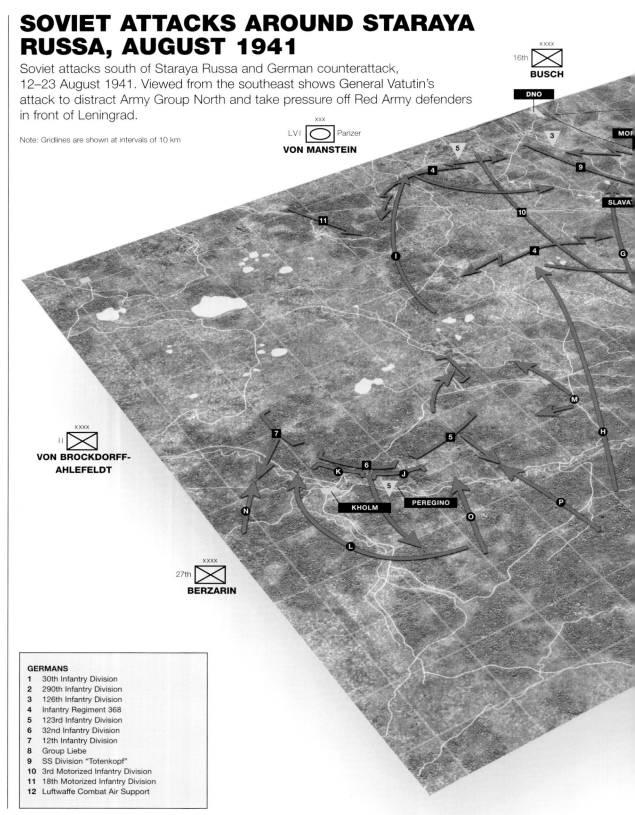

**GERMANS**

| | |
|---|---|
| 1 | 30th Infantry Division |
| 2 | 290th Infantry Division |
| 3 | 126th Infantry Division |
| 4 | Infantry Regiment 368 |
| 5 | 123rd Infantry Division |
| 6 | 32nd Infantry Division |
| 7 | 12th Infantry Division |
| 8 | Group Liebe |
| 9 | SS Division "Totenkopf" |
| 10 | 3rd Motorized Infantry Division |
| 11 | 18th Motorized Infantry Division |
| 12 | Luftwaffe Combat Air Support |

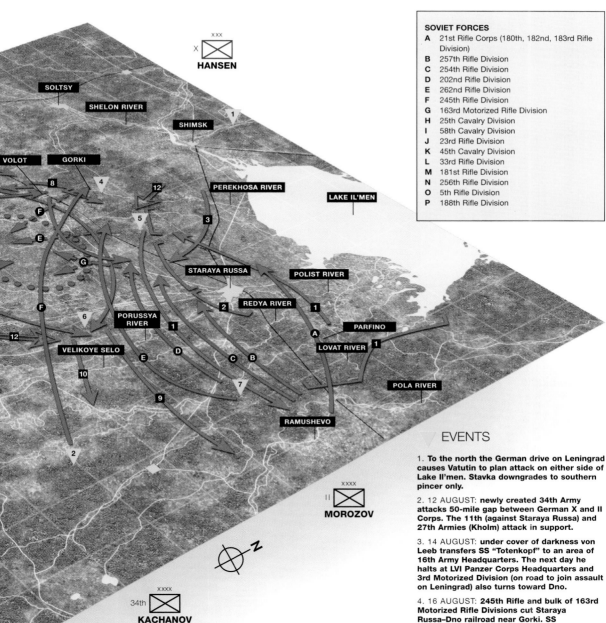

**SOVIET FORCES**

- **A** 21st Rifle Corps (180th, 182nd, 183rd Rifle Division)
- **B** 257th Rifle Division
- **C** 254th Rifle Division
- **D** 202nd Rifle Division
- **E** 262nd Rifle Division
- **F** 245th Rifle Division
- **G** 163rd Motorized Rifle Division
- **H** 25th Cavalry Division
- **I** 58th Cavalry Division
- **J** 23rd Rifle Division
- **K** 45th Cavalry Division
- **L** 33rd Rifle Division
- **M** 181st Rifle Division
- **N** 256th Rifle Division
- **O** 5th Rifle Division
- **P** 188th Rifle Division

HANSEN

SOLTSY

SHELON RIVER

SHIMSK

VOLOT    GORKI

PEREKHOSA RIVER

LAKE IL'MEN

STARAYA RUSSA

POLIST RIVER

REDYA RIVER

PORUSSYA RIVER

PARFINO

LOVAT RIVER

VELIKOYE SELO

POLA RIVER

RAMUSHEVO

MOROZOV

KACHANOV

34th

## ▽ EVENTS

**1.** **To the north the German drive on Leningrad causes Vatutin to plan attack on either side of Lake Il'men. Stavka downgrades to southern pincer only.**

**2. 12 AUGUST: newly created 34th Army attacks 50-mile gap between German X and II Corps. The 11th (against Staraya Russa) and 27th Armies (Kholm) attack in support.**

**3. 14 AUGUST: under cover of darkness von Leeb transfers SS "Totenkopf" to an area of 16th Army Headquarters. The next day he halts at LVI Panzer Corps Headquarters and 3rd Motorized Division (on road to join assault on Leningrad) also turns toward Dno.**

**4. 16 AUGUST: 245th Rifle and bulk of 163rd Motorized Rifle Divisions cut Staraya Russa–Dno railroad near Gorki. SS "Totenkopf" moves out against their left flank. 21st Rifle Corps elements enter Staraya Russa behind withdrawing 30th Infantry Division.**

**5. 19 AUGUST: Headquarters LVI Panzer Corps and 3rd Motorized Infantry Division begins counterattack; 30th Infantry Division transitions from defense to offense. II Corps attacks at Kholm.**

**6. 20 AUGUST: despite terrible weather, but with Luftwaffe close air support, SS "Totenkopf" and 3rd Motorized Divisions meet near Velikaya Selo and close trap on bulk of 163rd, 202nd, 245th, 262nd Rifle, and 25th Cavalry Divisions.**

**7. 23 AUGUST: the 16th Army restores Lovat River Line but drive on Leningrad has had to continue minus valuable armored and Luftwaffe elements.**

The thick forests, wet marshes, and primitive infrastructure encountered during the latter part of Operation Barbarossa constituted ideal terrain for the Red Army's cavalry. Their 25th and 27th Cavalry Divisions actively participated in the Staraya Russa and Tikhvin operations. (US National Archives)

An engine for a panzer is unloaded from a Ju-52. Difficult terrain and weather, poor roads, and increasing partisan activity made aerial resupply essential for Hoepner's panzer spearheads throughout Barbarossa. (US National Archives)

The closer von Leeb got to Leningrad the farther behind he left the Blitzkrieg. Early in Barbarossa, as a morale-boosting measure the men of 3rd Motorized Division were told they could grow beards until Leningrad fell. By late August commanders bowed to the inevitable and ordered their men to shave. Panzer thrusts, measured in hundreds of miles per month in June and July, now slowed to a crawl. German losses mounted: the 30th Infantry Division suffered 1,359 casualties during Barbarossa's first month, but 2,947 during the second. The Northwest Front suffered a bloodletting as well with: 25 of its 30 divisions at between 10 percent and 30 percent strength in July.

Von Leeb's repeated immobilization of Hoepner's panzers gave the Red Army time to strengthen its lines, even if only slightly. David Glantz has condemned this self-imposed surrender of the strategic initiative when Reinhardt stood practically unopposed on the Neva at Kingisepp, followed by continued inaction while the Sixteenth Army eliminated a tactical threat.

At Germany's highest level Hitler battled with his generals over Barbarossa's objectives. Between mid-July and mid-August Hitler issued four directives, but convincing the generals to follow them was another matter. Taking the unusual step of writing his own agitated *Denkschrift* (Study) on 22 August, the Führer finally settled the matter in his favor; with assistance from the Finns and Army Group Center, the capture of Leningrad would precede that of Moscow.

General Halder initially vigorously resisted reinforcing Army Group North with Hoth's panzers. Only when it was too late – and then in a piecemeal manner – did Halder relent. However, success was now less likely than weeks earlier. Even then the two Army Groups would not cooperate to liquidate a threat to their mutual flanks. By the time von Leeb had sufficient strength to either slaughter the Northwest Front or

**Red Army defenders of the Baltic Islands employing a 50mm M1940/1941 mortar. General Elisseyev and his men did not use the time between *Barbarossatag* and the German landings effectively and were essentially isolated from the remainder of the USSR. (History in the Making)**

***Pionier-Sturmboot 39* of the 61st Infantry Division crosses the sound between Estonia and Muhu Island on 14 September. German amphibious capabilities were severely tested during this one-division operation.**

# GERMAN JOINT ASSAULTS ON BALTIC ISLANDS, SEPTEMBER–OCTOBER 1941

Operation Beowulf II German joint assault on the Baltic Islands, 13 September–22 October 1941. Viewed from the southeast shows German Army, Kriegsmarine, Luftwaffe elements, and Brandenburg commandos attacking islands off the coast of Estonia to secure Baltic lines of communication.

Note: Gridlines are shown at intervals of 10 km

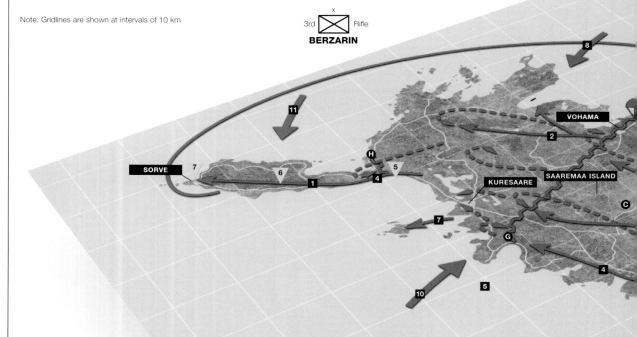

**BERZARIN**
3rd — Rifle

**GERMAN FORCES**

**Army**
1 Infantry Regiment 151
2 *Auflarungs Abteilung* 161
3 Infantry Regiment 176
4 Infantry Regiment 162
5 Motorized Group Sierigk
6 217th Infantry Division elements
7 Capture of Abro Island

**Naval**
8 Demonstration Westwind
9 Demonstration Nordwind
10 Demonstration Südwind
11 Operation West Storm
12 Operation East Prussia

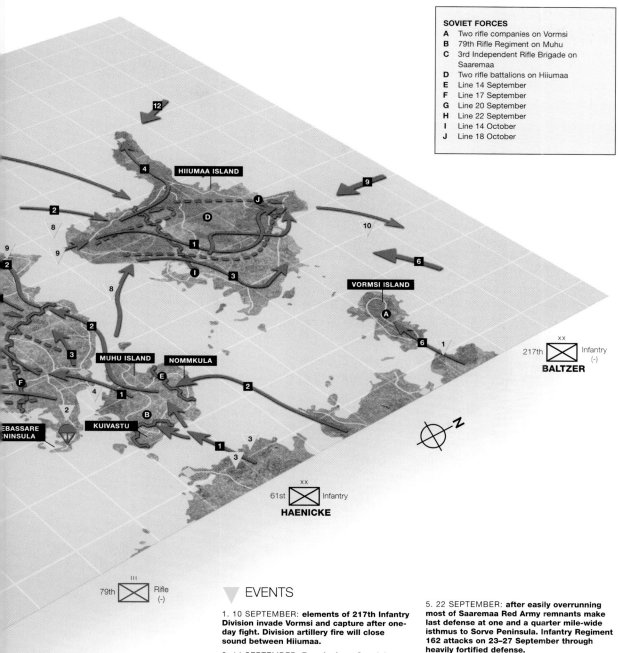

HIIUMAA ISLAND

VORMSI ISLAND

MUHU ISLAND    NOMMKULA

KUIVASTU

EBASSARE
NINSULA

217th  Infantry (-)
**BALTZER**

61st  Infantry
**HAENICKE**

79th  Rifle (-)

## ▼ EVENTS

1. 10 SEPTEMBER: **elements of 217th Infantry Division invade Vormsi and capture after one-day fight. Division artillery fire will close sound between Hiiumaa.**

2. 14 SEPTEMBER: **Brandenburg Special Command "Benesch" lands by glider near Soviet coastal battery in fort on Kuebassare Peninsula. Shipborne elements turned back by heavy seas.**

3. 14 SEPTEMBER: **Infantry Regiment 151 (in 180 boats) and *Auflarungs Abteilung* 161 (90 boats) cross from mainland to Muhu and manage to hold against uncoordinated Soviet counterattacks.**

4. MORNING OF 16 SEPTEMBER: **first elements of Infantry Regiment 151 then *Auflarungs Abteilung* 161 fight across two and a half mile-long causeway to Saaremaa against disorganized defense. Bridgehead secure by 1100 hours.**

5. 22 SEPTEMBER: **after easily overrunning most of Saaremaa Red Army remnants make last defense at one and a quarter mile-wide isthmus to Sorve Peninsula. Infantry Regiment 162 attacks on 23–27 September through heavily fortified defense.**

6. EVENING OF 27 SEPTEMBER: **Infantry Regiment 151, with the help of Luftwaffe close air support and naval gunfire, breeches Soviet defensive lines and captures Sorve Peninsula.**

7. 5 OCTOBER: **Soviets evacuate Sorve by sea; 1,500 soldiers escape to Hiiumaa.**

8. MORNING OF 12 OCTOBER: **Infantry Regiment 151 follows to Hiiumaa.**

9. AFTERNOON OF 12 OCTOBER: **IR 176 and AA161 conduct amphibious landing against south shore of Hiiumaa.**

10. 21–22 OCTOBER: **Soviets abandon Baltic Islands; 570 men manage to escape.**

61st Infantry Division soldiers in a rubber raft on Hiiumaa Island in October. Leading the group is an Unteroffizier (foreground) and a Leutnant behind him. Although the Baltic Islands were not large they had extensive areas of marshland. (History in the Making)

link up with Mannerheim the opportunity had passed. One can only guess whether another Kiev-style *Kessel* in the north might have been possible if the Germans had committed themselves fully.

# LENINGRAD, TIKHVIN AND VOLKHOV

Hitler saw St Petersburg, the seat of the Tsars, as a symbol of Russia's status as a great power, its dominance of Europe and its naval superiority in the Baltic Sea. His hatred of the renamed city of Leningrad as the cradle of Bolshevism was based on ideology and racism rather than strategy or politics. Vatutin's inconclusive Staraya Russa attack and the arrival of the XXXIX Panzer Corps sealed Leningrad's fate; if not captured outright the city would at the very least be a hostage of the Germans.

Von Leeb was optimistic about his army group's chances against the Red Army forces facing them, but Hitler was not. Reinhardt's Panzer Corps had been stalled within 100 miles of Leningrad since the first half of July. Now, nearly two months later the Germans anticipated the final assault on the city. On 4 September von Brauchitsch and Halder arrived at Army Group headquarters in Pskov. Keitel was already there and the three of them told von Leeb of his new mission: merely to surround Leningrad, not conquer it. The next day Hitler issued instructions giving von Leeb two missions: to encircle Leningrad by attacking toward Shlisselburg and also to drive on Volkhov in order to link up with the Finns on the Svir. On 6 September Hitler issued Führer Directive 35 dealing with the final attack on Moscow (Operation *Taifun*). This established 15 September as the date when *VIII Fliegerkorps* and Hoepner's remaining panzers would transfer to Army Group Center. In return von Leeb received the 7th Airborne Division flown in from Crete, the 250th Spanish "Blue" Division, plus the 212th and 227th Infantry Divisions from France.

Von Leeb's lack of focus on Leningrad would cost him his primary objective. All the while Mannerheim watched critically from Finland for any signs that Army Group North might falter as the United States and Soviet Union applied diplomatic pressure on his tiny nation to remain close to its 1939 borders.

### Resumption of the Assault on Leningrad

For a moment as the LVI Panzer moved north from Luga, Hoepner came close to building a two-panzer corps *Schwerpunkt* for the first time during Barbarossa. His superiors' overreaction to the Staraya Russa attack shattered that vision.

However, Reinhardt had not been idle during the Staraya Russa battles of the second half of August. The rain fell hard and the Red Army had turned most villages into fortresses. Soviet anti-tank mines reduced the ratio of destroyed panzers to Soviet tanks to 1:2 – a disastrous trend for the Germans. The German tank crews halted their advance periodically and assumed defensive *Igel*. So it continued for another week as 1st and 6th Panzer Divisions inched toward Krasnogvardeysk. On 24 August, XLI Panzer Corps reached the end of its endurance still short of the town, switching to a defensive posture for another two weeks.

Forces for the final assault of Leningrad lined up as follows. The *Schwerpunkt* under Hoepner consisted of the XLI Panzer and XXXVIII and L Army Corps with the missions of attacking Krasnogvardeysk and cutting off the 8th Army. Hoepner also commanded the XXVIII Army Corps and elements of the 12th Panzer Division on the Izhora, with Slutsk and Kolpino as their objectives. To the east stood Schmidt's XXXIX Panzer Corps (18th and 29th Motorized Divisions), which was to chase the Soviets away from Leningrad and prevent any relief efforts. On the Soviet Leningrad Front were the 8th Army to the west, the 42nd Army (Lieutenant General F.S. Ivanov) near Krasnogvardeysk and the 55th Army (Major General I.G. Lazarev) around Slutsk and Kolpino. The defenders numbered 452,000 men. Included in that number were 80,000 naval infantry in seven brigades. Popov at least had the flexibility to transfer forces from the 23rd Army in Karelia to more threatened sectors.

Army Group North's last effort to take Leningrad began on the eastern flank. Schmidt's Panzer Corps battled the 55th Army on its right and the 54th on its left as it made straight for Lake Ladoga via Chudovo, which fell on 25 August. The noose closed around Leningrad when Shlisselburg fell on 8 September. The hero of the moment was Lieutenant Colonel Harry Hoppe, the same man who captured Novgorod's Kremlin the month before. Voroshilov was afraid to tell Stalin of the disaster so the latter learned the bad news via German radio.

As temperatures dropped Reinhardt felt strong enough to attack at 0930hrs on 9 September. The 36th Motorized and 1st Panzer Divisions led the way through Krasnogvardeysk and the old Tsarist barracks at Dudergof, which fell on the 11th, but Hoepner had no reserve to exploit the success. A day later the 1st and 6th Panzer Divisions entered Leningrad's inner defensive ring near Krasnoye Selo. Under orders from Stalin not to surrender, Red Army soldiers blew themselves up with hand grenades rather than show the white flag. Stukas from von Richthofen's *VIII Fliegerkorps* dropped bombs 200–300 yards in front of the Germans. Meanwhile the XXVIII Corps and 55th Army fought to a draw near Slutsk.

Smelling another trap Hoepner released his new reserves, the 8th Panzer, to pass Reinhardt's right and then to swing south. It would

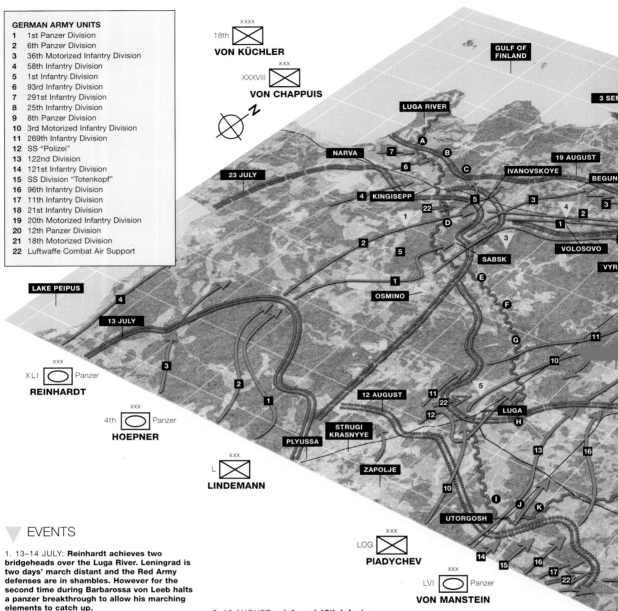

**GERMAN ARMY UNITS**
1   1st Panzer Division
2   6th Panzer Division
3   36th Motorized Infantry Division
4   58th Infantry Division
5   1st Infantry Division
6   93rd Infantry Division
7   291st Infantry Division
8   25th Infantry Division
9   8th Panzer Division
10  3rd Motorized Infantry Division
11  269th Infantry Division
12  SS "Polizei"
13  122nd Division
14  121st Infantry Division
15  SS Division "Totenkopf"
16  96th Infantry Division
17  11th Infantry Division
18  21st Infantry Division
19  20th Motorized Infantry Division
20  12th Panzer Division
21  18th Motorized Division
22  Luftwaffe Combat Air Support

18th VON KÜCHLER

XXXVIII VON CHAPPUIS

GULF OF FINLAND

LUGA RIVER

NARVA

23 JULY

IVANOVSKOYE

BEGUN

KINGISEPP

VOLOSOVO

VYR

SABSK

OSMINO

LAKE PEIPUS

13 JULY

XLI Panzer
REINHARDT

4th Panzer
HOEPNER

L
LINDEMANN

12 AUGUST

LUGA

STRUGI KRASNYYE

PLYUSSA

ZAPOLJE

UTORGOSH

LOG
PIADYCHEV

LVI Panzer
VON MANSTEIN

XXVIII
HOEP

3 SE

19 AUGUST

## ▼ EVENTS

**1. 13–14 JULY: Reinhardt achieves two bridgeheads over the Luga River. Leningrad is two days' march distant and the Red Army defenses are in shambles. However for the second time during Barbarossa von Leeb halts a panzer breakthrough to allow his marching elements to catch up.**

**2. 23 JULY: Piadyshev is removed from command of the Luga Operational Group (LOG) and arrested. The LOG is divided into Kingisepp, Luga, and Eastern sectors.**

**3. 8 AUGUST: 111th and 125th Rifle divisions attack the XLI Panzer Corps' bridgehead from the west.**

**4. 9–16 AUGUST: after three weeks in a costly defense, 1st and 6th Panzer Divisions attack to expand their bridgeheads in preparation for final assault on Leningrad.**

**5. 10–26 AUGUST: after numerous delays due to weather hampering Fliegerkorps VIII close air support, L Army Corps attacks against southern portion of Luga Line.**

**6. 15 AUGUST: XXXIX Panzer Corps transferred to Army Group North from Army Group Center. Its first action is attack on Lyuban on the 25th.**

**7. 16 AUGUST: reinforced 12th Infantry Division captures Novgorod Kremlin from 48th Army elements.**

**8. 19 AUGUST: the 8th Panzer Division veers southward from XLI Panzer attack to link up with L Army Corps coming north from Luga. Result is Army Group's largest Kessel, capturing nearly 20,000 Soviets from 41st Rifle Corps; closes on 30 August.**

**9. 21 AUGUST: L Army Corps captures Kranogvardiesk from 42nd Army.**

**10. 8 SEPTEMBER: 20th Motorized Infantry Division and other units capture Shlisselburg, isolating Leningrad from overland communications with remainder of the USSR. Beginning of 900-day siege.**

**11. 11 SEPTEMBER: final German assault on Leningrad begins. Dudergof Heights captured two days later. Essentially furthest advance toward Leningrad achieved by 24th.**

# BATTLE ON THE LUGA RIVER LINE AND APPROACHES TO LENINGRAD, AUGUST–SEPTEMBER 1941

The battle on the Luga River Line and the final German drive on Leningrad, August–September 1941. Viewed from the southeast, General Hoepner's Panzer Group had a bridgehead over the last major river before Leningrad exactly three weeks into Barbarossa but could not exploit success.

Note: Gridlines are shown at intervals of 20 km

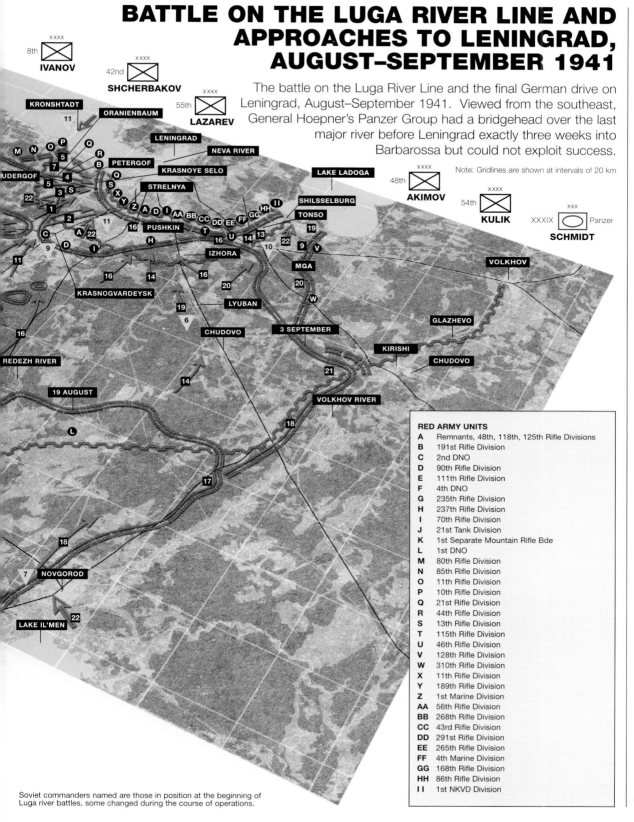

| RED ARMY UNITS | |
| --- | --- |
| A | Remnants, 48th, 118th, 125th Rifle Divisions |
| B | 191st Rifle Division |
| C | 2nd DNO |
| D | 90th Rifle Division |
| E | 111th Rifle Division |
| F | 4th DNO |
| G | 235th Rifle Division |
| H | 237th Rifle Division |
| I | 70th Rifle Division |
| J | 21st Tank Division |
| K | 1st Separate Mountain Rifle Bde |
| L | 1st DNO |
| M | 80th Rifle Division |
| N | 85th Rifle Division |
| O | 11th Rifle Division |
| P | 10th Rifle Division |
| Q | 21st Rifle Division |
| R | 44th Rifle Division |
| S | 13th Rifle Division |
| T | 115th Rifle Division |
| U | 46th Rifle Division |
| V | 128th Rifle Division |
| W | 310th Rifle Division |
| X | 11th Rifle Division |
| Y | 189th Rifle Division |
| Z | 1st Marine Division |
| AA | 56th Rifle Division |
| BB | 268th Rifle Division |
| CC | 43rd Rifle Division |
| DD | 291st Rifle Division |
| EE | 265th Rifle Division |
| FF | 4th Marine Division |
| GG | 168th Rifle Division |
| HH | 86th Rifle Division |
| II | 1st NKVD Division |

Soviet commanders named are those in position at the beginning of Luga river battles, some changed during the course of operations.

rendezvous with the new L Army Corps (269th Infantry and "Polizei" Divisions) coming up from the town of Luga, which had just fallen with the loss of another 16,000 Soviets. Together they encircled nine divisions of the LOG and 41st Rifle Corps, capturing 25,000 Soviets near Vyritsa. By mid-September the Luga defense line had ceased to exist, while the 48th Army could field only 6,235 men and 31 guns. Further German advances looked doubtful, however.

Hoepner and von Leeb labored under imminent high command threats to pull Fourth Panzer Group out of the Leningrad fight and send it to Moscow. The field marshal suffered from a fatal resignation ("I'm fighting a poor-man's war.") while the panzer commander wanted one last push. Command and control arrangements were far from satisfactory for Hoepner. He had limited authority over the XXXVIII Corps on the left (under the Eighteenth Army) and none over the XXXIX Panzer Corps on the far right. Von Leeb appears to have exercised little decisive leadership. Accordingly German attacks were slow getting started and poorly coordinated.

On 9 September, Zhukov arrived in embattled, encircled Leningrad and gave Voroshilov the following note from Stalin: "Hand over command of the Front to Zhukov and fly back to Moscow immediately …" Zhukov promptly countermanded his predecessor's orders to make preparations to demolish the city and to scuttle the Red Banner Fleet. He issued his own "not one step back" instructions and provided the defense with shape by creating his own main effort near Uritsk, sending reinforcements there and ordering counterattacks.

On 13 September, with the battle on a knife edge, Reinhardt committed the 1st Panzer, 36th Motorized, and 1st and 58th Infantry Divisions at Uritsk. A day later he ordered the 6th Panzer (by now down to 9,000 men) to Pushkin and sent 8th Panzer to assist Schmidt to the east. As often happened, these assaults preempted a move planned by Zhukov. Close to the center of the line, the 121st Infantry Division, with many elements at one third strength, battled in the "haunted" forests. They could see the golden cupolas and towers of Leningrad a mere dozen miles away. Toward the end of the month both sides settled down to an active defense and began a propaganda war using loudspeakers.

Hoepner's men wondered if this was the final assault. Their high-water mark came on 18 September as the XXVIII Corps took Slutsk while the 1st Panzer and "Polizei" Divisions took Pushkin, with 1st Panzer engaging new tanks fresh from the factory at Kolpino. That same day, however, the 6th Panzer received orders to pull out and make for Moscow, followed on the 20th by the remainder of XLI Panzer Corps.

To the west, on 16 September Reinhardt's men reached the Gulf of Finland at Strelnya, isolating Major General Cherbakov's 8th Army from Leningrad. To the east, 54th Army attacks at Mga failed to dislodge the XXXIX Panzer Corps. The main defense in Leningrad's suburbs began to gel around this time. The 1st Panzer halted at the high-water mark of White Russian forces during the Civil War and by 25 September the front lines had solidified.

With that, 900 days of darkness descended over Leningrad while the moon circled like a vulture; 1,000,000 citizens starved in that first winter alone. Leningrad had been a frontline city during the Winter War but this would be different. The supplement to Führer Directive 33 advocated

**Spanish volunteers from the 250th "Blue" Infantry Division, in this case former students from Valencia, photographed on 18 September. The Spanish fought bravely in the Army Group North sector until as late as 1944. (US National Archives)**

Soviet POWs await their fate near the lower Luga River sector. With a smaller panzer group, Army Group North failed to achieve the massive encirclements that characterized the battles in the Army Group Center and Army Group South sectors. (US National Archives)

Pioneers of the XXVIII Army Corps assault Red Army fortifications near Slutsk on 15 September with a combination of flame throwers and explosives (note the pouches worn by three of the four men at left). This effectively marked the high-water mark of Army Group North's campaign. (History in the Making)

terror "to discourage any flicker of resistance" within the city. On 16 September Hitler stated "The venomous nest Petersburg out of which Asiatic poison so long gushed into the Baltic Sea would disappear from the face of the earth." A directive of 22 September, exactly three months after *Barbarossatag*, made his bombast official but no closer to realization.

Surrounding and starving Leningrad was only one option considered by Hitler; another would be to allow the United States to supply or evacuate the population. Toward the end of World War I General Erich Ludendorff wrote a study on the difficulties of taking St Petersburg, but naturally he was considering the implications of feeding its 2,000,000 people. Hitler was not constrained by similar humanitarian issues. On 10 September von Leeb asked what would be expected if women and children sought to escape starvation by coming through the German cordon. The Führer said, "They'd be shot." Von Leeb replied, "That might happen once, but no more. German soldiers don't shoot women and children … that would

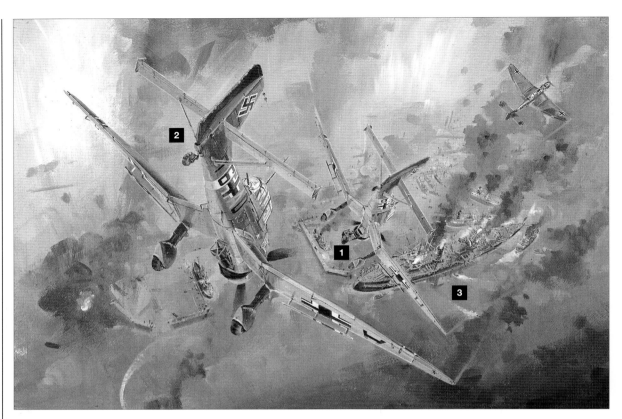

## HANS ULRICH RUDEL SINKS BATTLESHIP *MARAT* AT KRONSHTADT, 21 SEPTEMBER, 1941 (pages 80–81)

The Red Banner Baltic Fleet's home base on Kronshtadt Island near Leningrad represented a major German objective from Barbarossa's inception. Nazi Germany depended heavily on strategic materials from Sweden and Finland shipped across the Baltic. Hitler knew that if his advancing army could deprive the fleet of its bases, Admiral Tributs would basically have three options: scuttle the fleet, seek internment in neutral Sweden, or escape the narrow Baltic. The large Baltic Fleet became even more of a threat after gaining numerous forward operating bases when the USSR annexed the Baltic states in 1940. Hitler still had faith in the ability of his Luftwaffe and Kriegsmarine to handle the Soviets. However, less than a month prior to *Barbarossatag* the naval correlation of forces changed drastically when the Royal Navy sank the *Bismarck* in the North Atlantic. Admiral Tributs took precautions immediately before 22 June: including his dispatch of the battleship *Marat* from Tallinn to Kronshtadt with its awesome flak protection. Indeed, von Leeb's Army Group moved up the Baltic coast, gobbling Soviet bases at Libau and Riga. The naval situation altered markedly in the Germans' favor on 28 August when the 61st Infantry Division took Tallinn, the Red Banner Fleet's last base out side of Kronshtadt. The Soviet evacuation was a disaster: the Germans destroyed 25 percent of vessels participating and the Soviets lost 40 percent of passengers embarked. While German advances on the ground boxed in Tributs' fleet, it was nevertheless well placed to influence the battle now taking place around Leningrad. Kronshtadt lay less than ten miles from the mainland and Soviet warships could provide supporting fire to Red Army forces from their piers. By mid-September Hitler worried that the Soviet ships would break out to the Atlantic while army commanders complained about the naval gunfire. The Führer ordered his own commander in the Baltic to create a force centered on the Tirpitz to terminate the Red Banner Fleet. The Luftwaffe acted first, however. The task fell to Stukageschwader 2, "Immelmann." At Kronshtadt stood two battleships, two cruisers, 13 destroyers, and more than 200 other vessels guarded by over 600 anti-aircraft guns – 50 battalions' worth. Flak explodes while the Stukas are still ten miles out. Starting at 9,000 feet altitude the dive bombers tip over for the final run. They carry 2,000-pound bombs especially made for large warships (1). Planes are nearly wingtip to wingtip and so close behind one another that there is a danger of ramming. Pilots plunge at about 80° without using dive brakes in order to get through the bursting artillery. Lieutenant Hans Ulrich Rudel (T6+AD) (2) keeps his sights on the *Marat* (3). He pushes the bomb release then pulls back on the stick. He momentarily blacks out from the G-force until his radioman/gunner tells him "She is blowing up, sir!" "Immelmann" returned to Kronshtadt and severely damaged the cruisers *Kirov* and *Maxim Gorki* but had less success against the battleship *Oktyabruskaya Revolutsia*. However, Rudel and his comrades won an incomplete victory; the crippled *Marat* settled into the shallow water of the bay, but her stern guns continued to bombard German soldiers on the mainland preparing their final assaults on Leningrad. (Howard Gerrard)

**Mounted reconnaissance elements of the 1st Infantry Division approaching Kronshtadt Bay in September. This maneuver isolated remnants of the Soviet 8th Army at Oranienbaum until 1944. (History in the Making)**

cause a severe crisis in discipline." The field marshal was obviously naive about what German soldiers would or would not do during the Nazi–Soviet war. However his point was evidently lost on Hitler.

In any event the issue never arose. For his part, on 21 September Stalin also issued draconian orders concerning Leningrad. The USSR would re-supply the city and the population would manage as best it could. Because Hitler halted his forces so early and Finland refused to be drawn into a fight for the huge metropolis, Leningrad maintained a substantial hinterland of over 1,100 square miles. That space provided ample room for troop concentrations, airfields, depots, and factories, which dissipated the Luftwaffe's effectiveness. In fact, industry continued to produce ammunition, weapons, and vehicles – and repaired much of the same – out of the range of German artillery. Finally, due to the city's stout air defenses, the Luftwaffe bombardment lasted barely two weeks in September.

### Tikhvin and Volkhov

As the final assault on Leningrad played itself out, Stavka took seriously the threat that Army Group North might manage to link up with the Finns. To reinforce the 7th Independent Army now resting on the Svir River, it established the 54th, 52nd, and 4th Armies in or near Volkhov. It shifted one tank and eight rifle divisions to the sector. German reinforcements during the same period consisted of the 254th Infantry Division at Volkhov and the 61st at Tikhvin. However, Hitler remained unmoved. Though he only had the battered XXXIX Panzer Corps left for such a mission, he ordered an attack northward. Stalin also urged his commanders to attack to re-open communications with Leningrad. Marshal G.I. Kulik assembled 63,000 men in eight divisions supported by 475 guns and 59 new KV tanks to attack on 20 October.

Typically, the Germans moved more quickly than the Soviets and struck on the 16th. While General Schmidt left to temporarily replace the ill commander of the Second Army, the XXXIX Panzer, presently under General of Panzer Troops Hans-Jurgen von Arnim, split the boundary between the 52nd and 4th Armies. Both sides fought hard for small villages to gain some shelter at night. Freezing weather caused a holocaust of horses, breaking the hearts of hardened *Landsers* at the suffering of their

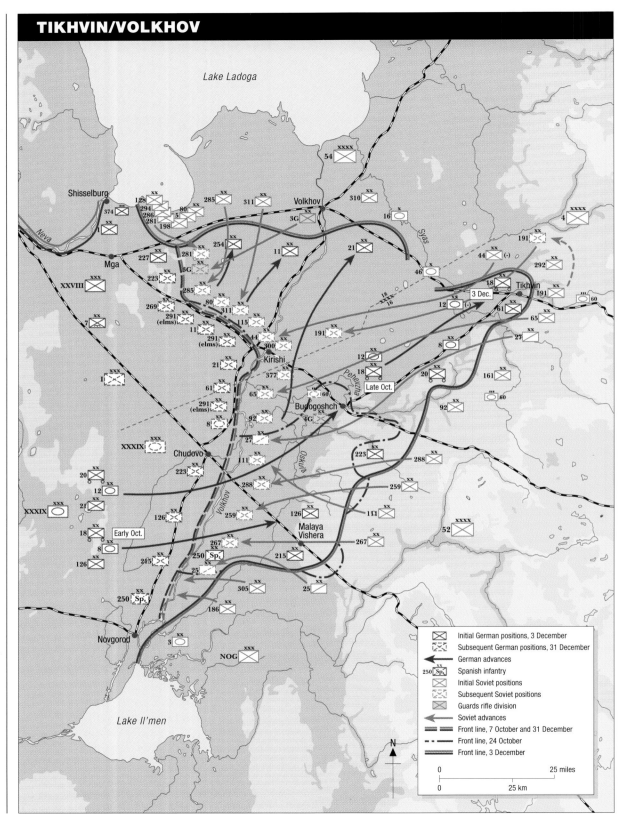

Lake Ladoga

Shisselburg

Mga

XXVIII

Volkhov

Syas

Tikhvin

3 Dec.

Late Oct.

Kirishi

Budogoshch

Pcheuzha

Oskuya

Chudovo

Early Oct.

Malaya Vishera

Novgorod

Lake Il'men

NOG

N

| | |
|---|---|
| Initial German positions, 3 December | |
| Subsequent German positions, 31 December | |
| German advances | |
| Spanish infantry | 250 Sp. |
| Initial Soviet positions | |
| Subsequent Soviet positions | |
| Guards rifle division | |
| Soviet advances | |
| Front line, 7 October and 31 December | |
| Front line, 24 October | |
| Front line, 3 December | |

0 — 25 miles

0 — 25 km

A rather idyllic-looking street scene in a town obviously left unscathed by the ravages of Barbarossa. German soldiers and convoys intermingle with native townspeople and sledges. Hitler's plans for a subdued Leningrad were not so harmonious. (History in the Making)

equine companions. With 12th Panzer and 18th and 20th Motorized Divisions leading the way, the Germans captured Mal Vishera within one week. The German advance stopped and started as the weather in turn thawed and froze the mud and ice amid terrain cluttered with forests, lakes, and swamps. On 26 October von Leeb flew to Führer Headquarters in a vain attempt to squeeze additional support from the dictator. Henceforth, the field marshal described successive attacking forces simply as "new victims." Nevertheless the Germans crawled forward against the collapsing defense. Finally the Germans occupied Tikhvin on 8 November. Approximately 20,000 POWs, 179 guns, and 96 tanks fell into their hands.

From then on the 126th Infantry, 20th Motorized, and 8th Panzer Divisions (all very weak) attempted to defend 60 miles of front in an exposed salient. Although *Luftwaffekommando Tikhvin* (KG 77 and II/JG 54) provided some air cover, despite miserable weather, the Germans reaped no benefit from their brief occupation of Tikhvin's bauxite mines. To the northeast Group Boeckmann (I Army Corps, 11th and 21st Infantry Divisions, reinforced by the 254th) pushed to within four miles of Volkhov.

Tikhvin's beaten defenders fled and threatened to rout into the rear of the 7th Army facing the Finns. Kulik relinquished command and was soon executed. Stalin put 7th Army commander General K.A. Meretskov (just released from NKVD prison) in charge of the shaky 4th Army as well, with instructions to get positive control of the situation.

\* \* \*

Stalin resolved to take the offensive along the entire front. With the Wehrmacht's main striking forces concentrated around Moscow, he would attack on the two flanks. Marshal Timoshenko would lead the assault in the south around Rostov. In the north the Germans' vulnerable salient at Tikhvin looked like a target of opportunity. According to Stavka's plan the 54th Army (Lieutenant General I.I. Fedyuninsky) would attack around Volkhov, the 4th under Meretskov would reduce the Tikhvin salient as the main effort and the 52nd

A column of Stoewer light cross-country vehicles negotiate muddy roads and thick forests near Demyansk in September. As the German advance pressed further from the Soviet border, so the transport infrastructure became increasingly primitive. (History in the Making)

(Lieutenant General N.K. Klykov) plus the Novgorod Operational Group would advance in the south. Their overall goal was nothing less than reopening the Tihkvin–Leningrad railway and the destruction of all German forces east of the Volkhov River. At one point during the second half of October, Luftwaffe reconnaissance noted about 2,000 vehicles reinforcing the Volkhov Front.

The Red Army intentionally used staggered starts for its attacks. The 52nd Army began in the south on 12 November, with Meretskov launching the primary assault on the 19th. The 52nd Army's attack produced meager results but forced the Germans to react by committing reserves. In the center Meretskov caused von Leeb the most concern. As the latter noted in his diary on 22 November, "Tikhvin is more or less encircled." He knew he had to assemble a counterattack force and regain the town. The best he could do was rush in Haenicke's much-traveled 61st Infantry Division.

Some 28 German divisions faced 75 Soviet, many of the latter fresh. By 3 December, XXXIX Panzer Corps reported it could no longer defend Tikhvin against the 4th Army. On the 6th Hitler still insisted the town be held, but the very next day von Leeb told the 61st Infantry to prepare to withdraw. That same night, 7 December, he authorized the town's evacuation, telling the Führer over the phone of his "very painful duty to report that Tikhvin, over which we've fought and occupied for weeks, must regrettably be given up." Hitler approved the move *post facto* at 0200hrs the next morning.

Near Volkhov the Soviet 54th Army drove the I Army Corps south before it. A general withdrawal began as the Red Army hounded German rearguards. By mid-December Army Group North was back on the Volkhov River, where it had been two months earlier. Von Leeb tried to put a good face on his men's accomplishments during Barbarossa in his Christmas Order of the Day: 438,950 POWs, 4,590 guns, and 3,847 tanks captured or destroyed in five months. However, it was clear to all that the invasion, begun with such high hopes in June, had culminated without Army Group North accomplishing its objectives.

Whether Army Group North could have conquered Leningrad is one of history's unknowns. The question is also largely academic – the fact is that Hitler ordered von Leeb's men to halt short of the city. Throughout the campaign, practically every time the army group, and usually more specifically Hoepner's panzers, was on the brink of success a higher headquarters halted them for the infantry or logistics to catch up. These pauses resulted in a fatal loss of momentum that allowed the Soviets time to recover. Halder had lost the Byzantine battle within Führer Headquarters over reinforcing Army Group South with Guderian's Second Panzer Group, but as a result he dug in his heels against sending Hoth's panzers north to von Leeb. Halder's "victory" undermined Barbarossa in the north.

The decision to halt von Leeb outside of Leningrad doubtless saved his men from desperate and bitter urban warfare, but it also left the army group holding a long front line that made heavy manpower demands. As a result, investing Leningrad tied down too great a proportion of the army group's strength and left it with no reserves. The Red Air Force and its anti-aircraft artillery ruled the skies over the city while "almost the entire generation of [Luftwaffe] prewar trained officers was lost in combat."[4]

Although in command at Leningrad for less than a month, Zhukov arrived at the critical point. He conducted an active defense, fired weak commanders, and forbade further retreat. For their part, the Germans were never able to completely seal off the city from the rest of the USSR. Bombing Lake Ladoga's thick ice in order to cut the supply road, for example, was an exercise in futility; Soviet truck drivers easily drove around any holes, which re-froze quickly in any event. Wehrmacht soldiers also could not contend well with the elements; even Spanish dictator Francisco Franco took better care to feed and clothe his *Guripas* warmly than Hitler did his *Landsers*.

Finland always had limited objectives for the war and Mannerheim took a dim view of the Germans' demonstrated weakness in front of Leningrad. As the Red Army drove Army Group North away from Tikhvin and Volkhov after only a month, the prospect of the two Axis allies linking up receded yet further. In the final analysis, the Wehrmacht's half measures at Tikhvin and Volkhov only drained valuable resources from the *Ostheer's* Moscow *Schwerpunkt*.

---

4 Bergstrom, *Black Cross, Red Star*, p. 222

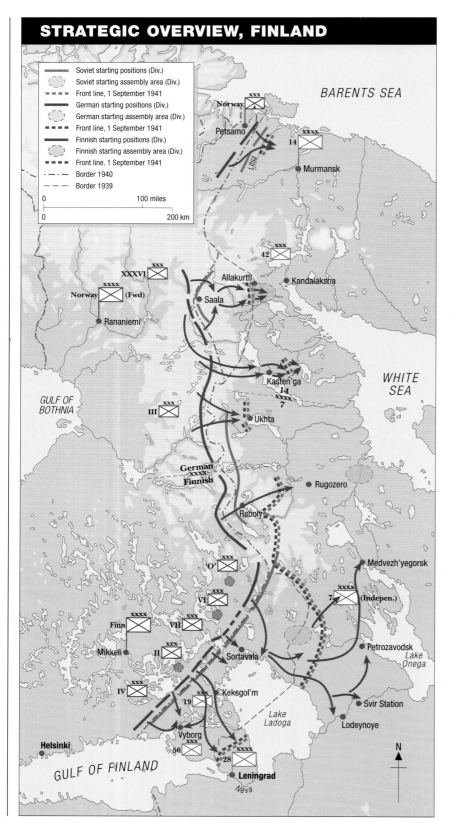

Legend:
- Soviet starting positions (Div.)
- Soviet starting assembly area (Div.)
- Front line, 1 September 1941
- German starting positions (Div.)
- German starting assembly area (Div.)
- Front line, 1 September 1941
- Finnish starting positions (Div.)
- Finnish starting assembly area (Div.)
- Front line, 1 September 1941
- Border 1940
- Border 1939

0 ———— 100 miles
0 ———— 200 km

BARENTS SEA

Norway XXX
Petsamo
Litsa
14 XXXX
Murmansk

42 XXX
XXXVI XXX
Norway XXXX (Fwd)
Allakurtti
Kandalaksha
Saala
Rananiemi

III XXX
Kasten'ga
14 XXXX
7
WHITE SEA
Ukhta

German XXXX Finnish

Rugozero
Reboly

'O' XXX
Medvezh'yegorsk
VI XXX
7 XXXX (Indepen.)
Finn XXXX
VII XXX
Mikkeli
II XXX
Petrozavodsk
Lake Onega
Sortavala
IV XXX
Keksgol'm
19 XXX
Lake Ladoga
Svir Station
Vyborg XXX
Lodeynoye
50 XXX
28 XXXX
Helsinki
Leningrad
Neva
GULF OF FINLAND
GULF OF BOTHNIA

N

Panzerbefehlswagen Ausf F or H with both the original tubular aerial plus the newer telescoping type with guy-wires. Neither aerial was very practical but sufficed to give the Germans superior tactical command and control. (History in the Making)

# CONCLUSIONS

**T**hree weeks after issuing his Order of the Day on 25 December, von Leeb asked that, due to the supply situation and the "railroad catastrophe," Army Group North be allowed to withdraw to its depots. Hitler ordered him to stand fast. During a 1½-hour telephone conversation on 13 January the field marshal asked Hitler to replace him with a younger man. The Führer refused. Over the following two days the situation deteriorated and he released von Leeb from command on the 16th. On the next day Busch took over Army Group North.

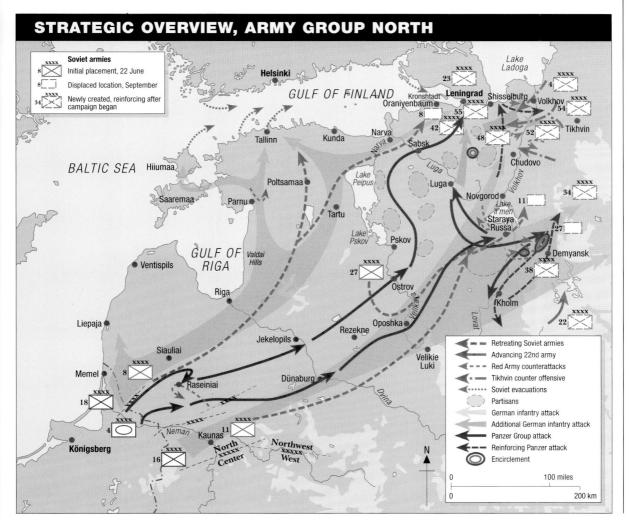

## STRATEGIC OVERVIEW, ARMY GROUP NORTH

**Soviet armies**

8 ⊠ Initial placement, 22 June

8 ⊡ Displaced location, September

34 ⊠ Newly created, reinforcing after campaign began

◄--- Retreating Soviet armies
◄━━ Advancing 22nd army
◄--- Red Army counterattacks
◄-·-· Tikhvin counter offensive
····· Soviet evacuations
⬭ Partisans
⬛ German infantry attack
⬛ Additional German infantry attack
◄━ Panzer Group attack
◄--- Reinforcing Panzer attack
◎ Encirclement

0 ____ 100 miles
0 ____ 200 km

N

This Obergefreiter (left) and a private have dug in beside a destroyed T-34. Amongst the clutter of their fighting position can be seen Kar 98 carbines, an MG34, a bayonet, cooking equipment, and an M1938 gas mask canister. (US National Archives)

Field Marshal von Leeb conducted a flawed campaign. As he said later he had "very limited experience in the use of panzer formations on a large scale." This was quite obvious as at numerous critical junctures he halted Hoepner or refused to accept the risks essential to Blitzkrieg success. He failed to stand up to his higher headquarters' demands that he divide Fourth Panzer Group into non-mutually supporting corps; in an analogous situation in the Ukraine, Field Marshal Gerd von Rundstedt refused to break up von Kleist's panzers as OKH demanded. As Army Group North commander, the lion's share of its failings rest on von Leeb's shoulders.

Of course, like all Barbarossa commanders, he was saddled with a flawed plan and capricious strategic leadership. As one Luftwaffe general wrote after the war, the German plan "was not based on meticulous and detailed planning by the German General Staff, but centered on a number of general directives issued by Hitler …"[5] The issue of Barbarossa's *Schwerpunkt* had been ignored in Führer Directive 21 and had to be addressed one month into the campaign, a wrangle that took over a month to settle.

The plan also hinged on ideology wedded to an exaggerated opinion of the Wehrmacht's strengths and Soviet weaknesses. The plan's cornerstone was its abysmal intelligence estimate of the Red Army. German intelligence knew very little about their future enemy despite ten years' efforts. In addition, every *Abwehr* (counterintelligence) agent in the USSR had been turned. The only decent intelligence the Germans received came courtesy of their signal intercept services. Von Leeb's own operational level plan did not take into account the fact that with such a small panzer group its only hope of encircling and destroying major portions of the Red Army would be to trap the enemy against the Baltic Sea.

**5** Hermann Plocher, *German Air Force versus Russia*, p. xi

Bf 109F of II/JG-53 *Pik As* (Ace of Spades) on an Estonian airfield alongside the burnt-out shell of a Red Air Force Polikarpov fighter. Except when reinforced by *VIII Fliegerkorps*, *Luftflotte 1* was another formation trying to fight Barbarossa on a shoe-string, much to the Army's frustration. (History in the Making)

Similarly, in common with other commanders von Leeb wielded an imperfect weapon. The Wehrmacht's leadership might have gained some valuable tactical lessons from the 1940 Western campaign, but it had learned all the wrong operational and strategic ones. In von Leeb's case he labored with an undersized contingent of panzers. He had the same marching and horse-drawn infantry divisions as the rest of the *Ostheer*, basically unchanged since 1918. At one point during Barbarossa two thirds of the German infantry divisions considered significantly under strength belonged to Army Group North.

The Luftwaffe still tried to prosecute a reduced war against Britain, had no reserves to speak of, had sent training units into combat as a short-term solution to its small size, and soon lost invaluable specialists. It concentrated its efforts only twice during Barbarossa, once at the battles against the Luga River line preparatory to attacking Leningrad. The Luftwaffe's premier close air support unit, *VIII Fliegerkorps*, deployed only when approved by Göring and Hitler. Its commander, von Richthofen, was very critical of von Leeb's campaign. The Luftwaffe flew without rest throughout the battles in the north: it supported the advance to the Dvina River, attacked Kronstadt and Murmansk naval bases, and mined numerous harbors, attacked the Stalin Line and the White Sea (Stalin) Canal, supported the Staraya Russa defense and counterattack, the advance on Leningrad, amphibious operations against the Baltic Islands, and the defense at Tikhvin all the while interdicting Soviet rail lines throughout the theater.

Nevertheless Army Group North began the invasion very well. Führer Headquarters viewed its initial reports with disbelief. Von Leeb could not manage conflicting reports from below and conflicting orders from above. Mismanaged victories, such as at Dünaburg, were often repeated. Neither was von Leeb the right man to command the Leningrad effort during the leadership vacuum represented by the Hitler–Halder duel in mid-summer. Von Leeb eventually received two panzer corps from Hoth, separated by time and space. Without the mass of a similar reorganization to that which sent Guderian southward, the impact of the additional panzers on Army Group North was significantly less. The former maneuver created the largest encirclement battle in history while the latter is practically forgotten.

In Finland the Axis tried in vain to fight an effective campaign in a poorly resourced strategic backwater. Von Falkenhorst constantly worried about Hitler's emphasis on defending Norway and fought with too little, directed from too far away. Hitler had no respect for the 60 miles Dietl had to cover to reach Murmansk. Mannerheim's Finns outclassed the Soviets at every turn but were not fighting a war for world domination like Germany. The possibility of Finland also involved in an unlimited war would completely change the complexion of Barbarossa in the north, but this prospect properly belongs in the category of historical fiction.

The poor leadership of first Kuznetsov and then Voroshilov presented von Leeb with every opportunity to succeed in the early stages. While the Red Army may have collapsed along the northern front, the Soviet state held strong everywhere; Stalin's USSR was internally stable. The Northwest Front may not have halted Army Group North, but it did cause von Leeb to swerve more than once. Counterattacks at Soltsy and Staraya Russa might have failed tactically, or even operationally, but succeeded at the strategic level.

The battle for Leningrad magnified differences in leadership on both sides. Von Leeb could not focus his strength on a single, decisive *Schwerpunkt*. Across the front lines, however, Zhukov brought superior command to bear. Even though the Germans cut off Leningrad from overland communication with Moscow eight days before Zhukov's arrival this did not signify the end of the city's struggle. The fact that Leningrad did not surrender when essentially surrounded, and indeed never would capitulate, was undoubtedly a bad omen for Germans hoping for a quick victory at Moscow. Both huge cities were central to the Soviet state, and cities that it was prepared to die fighting for.

Von Leeb told the postwar Nuremberg tribunal he "hardly hoped ever to reach the gates of Leningrad." General Günther Blumentritt, writing after the war, compared Hitler's decision to halt before taking the city to a similar decision at Dunkirk 16 months earlier. Blumentritt believed that Leningrad "probably would have fallen." However, as he would do weeks later, when declaring the battle for Moscow over following the twin encirclements at Bryansk and Vyazma, Hitler announced victory too soon. Simply butchering the population of Leningrad, even in the irrational world of the Third Reich does not seem a likely course of action even if the city capitulated. Slaughter was obviously on Hitler's mind. Exploitation and extermination of conquered peoples may have appealed to some in the Nazi hierarchy as a solution during a quick Blitzkrieg. Moral questions aside, this was no way to fight a world war of attrition where every ally was critical. But by the end of Barbarossa it was too late for the Germans to change their behavior, even had they been so inclined.

With Paulus admittedly concerned about purely military issues, Hitler was left to be his "own Ludendorff" and run the political and economic aspects of the Nazi–Soviet War. Key generals like Halder would not accede to the Führer's primacy, however. In addition to fighting the stubborn Stalin, Hitler had to struggle with his own general staff while the Red Army essentially bled white and demechanized the *Ostheer*. Combined with the wrong man at the top, Army Group North had to conduct a flawless campaign if it hoped to succeed. This was an unrealistic expectation that it failed to achieve.

# THE BATTLEFIELD TODAY

| German | Baltic/Russian |
|--------|----------------|
| Arensburg | Kuresaare |
| Dägo Is. | Hiiumaa |
| Dorpat | Tartu |
| Düna River | Daugava/Dvina |
| Dünaburg | Daugavpils/Dvinsk |
| Fellin | Viljandi |
| Jacobstadt | Jekolopils |
| Jamburg | Kingisepp |
| Libau | Liepaja |
| Memel | Klaipeda |
| Memel River | Nemunas/Niemen |
| Mitau | Jelgava |
| Moon Island | Muhu |
| Oberpahlen | Poltsamaa |
| Ösel Island | Saaremaa |
| Pernau | Pärnu |
| Pleskau | Pskov |
| Reval | Tallinn |
| Rositten | Rezekne |
| Schaulen | Siauliai |
| Tauroggen | Taurage |
| Weissenstein | Paide |
| Wesenburg | Rakvere |
| Wilkomierz | Ukmerge |

Visiting the battlefields discussed in this book is often more an adventure than tourism. In the Baltic states democratization, the rule of law, and integration into the European Union (EU) have made visiting increasingly easy. Traveling with a native speaker is always best. However, although Russian is still the most widely used alternative language, English is becoming more common, especially in larger cities and in businesses (hotels, restaurants, etc) catering to westerners. Driving to obscure battlefields can be exciting, considering indifferent signage and narrow country roads, but gas stations accepting major credit and ATM cards are plentiful. Finland (an EU member since 1995) has the amenities one would expect in Scandinavia.

Northwestern Russia, especially St Petersburg, is a popular tourist destination. Modern "St Pete" is searching for a new identity after centuries as Tsarist Russia's "Window to the World" and decades as the USSR's revolutionary birthplace. The "Monument to the Heroic Defenders of Leningrad" including an exhibit chronicling the 900-Day Siege lies part way between the airport and city center. The region also includes Novgorod's Kremlin and churches, and Staraya Russa's Dostoyevsky museum. Unlike EU countries, however, a tourist visa is presently required to enter Russia.

Monuments to World War II are generally of the "tank on a pedestal with a plaque" variety. Locales suffered different amounts of damage and have recovered in different ways. In Lithuania, for example, while Vilnius retains the look and feel of a historic Baltic city, Kaunas was rebuilt in the drab Soviet postwar style. There are numerous ways of traveling to the area. Cruise ships call at a variety of ports along the Baltic Sea coast, and Helsinki, St Petersburg and Warsaw airports handle many daily flights from the West.

\* \* \*

Place names mentioned in this volume have changed over the centuries due to conquest, treaty, statehood, and a variety of other influences. Often, a town or city may have an indigenous Baltic, a German, and a Russian name. Different documents, books or maps may use different names for the same place. The concordance to the left is provided to help the reader with the sometimes complex task of identification.

# BIBLIOGRAPHY

Bergstrom, Christer, and Andrey Mikhailov, *Black Cross, Red Star*, Pacifica Military History, 2000

Boog, Horst, ed., "Attack on the Soviet Union," *Germany and the Second World War*, Vol. IV, Clarendon Press, 1998

Buxa, Werner, *Weg und Schicksal der 11. Infanterie-Division*, Podzun Verlag, 1963

Carell, Paul, *Hitler Moves East*, Ballantine, 1971

Chales de Beaulieu, Walter, *Der Vorstoss der Panzergruppe 4 auf Leningrad-1941*, Scharnhorst, 1961

Clark, Alan, *Barbarossa*, William Morrow, 1965

Creveld, Martin van, *Supplying War*, Cambridge University, 1977

Creveld, Martin van, ed., *Airpower and Maneuver Warfare*, Air University Press, 1994

Dieckhoff, Gerhard, *Die 3. Infanterie-Division*, H.W. Blick, 1960

Ellis, John, *Brute Force*, Viking, 1990

English, John, *On Infantry*, Praeger, 1984

Erickson, John, *Road to Stalingrad*, Westview Press, 1984

Erickson, John, and David Dilks, eds, *Barbarossa*, Edinburgh University Press, 1994

Fugate, Bryan, *Operation Barbarossa*, Presidio Press, 1984

Glantz, David, ed., *The Initial Period of the War on the East Front, 22 June-August 1941*, Frank Cass, 1993

Glantz, David, and Jonathan House, *When Titans Clashed*, University of Kansas, 1995

Glantz, David, *Barbarossa*, Tempus, 2001

Goerlitz, Walter, *Paulus and Stalingrad*, Greenwood, 1974

Haupt, Werner, *Army Group North*, Schiffer Military History, 1997

Hubatsch, Walter, *Die 61. Infanterie-Division*, Podzun, 1983

Jentz, Thomas, ed., *Panzertruppen*, Schiffer Military History,1996

Kaltenegger, Roland, *Krieg am Eismeer*, Leopold Stocker, 1999

Kleinfeld, Gerald, and Lewis Tambs, *Hitler's Spanish Legion*, Southern Illinois University Press, 1979

Lewis, S.J., *Forgotten Legions*, Praeger, 1985

Lossberg, Bernhard von, *In Wehrmachtführungsstab*, H.H. Noelke, 1950

Luttichau, Charles von, unpublished manuscript

Manstein, Erich von, *Lost Victories*, Presidio, 1984

Manstein, Ruediger von, *Manstein*, Bernard & Graefe, 1981

Megargee, Geoffrey, *Inside Hitler's High Command*, University of Kansas, 2000

Meyer, Georg, ed., *Generalfeldmarschall Wilhelm Ritter von Leeb*, Beitrage zur Militaer und Kriegsgeschichte, 1976

Moynahan, Brian, *Claws of the Bear*, Houghton-Mifflin, 1989

Muller, Richard, *German Air War in Russia*, Nautical and Aviation Publishers of America, 1992

Nafziger, George, *German Order of Battle* Stackpole Books, 1999

Paul, Wolfgang, *Brennpunkte*, Hoentges Verlag, 1977

Plocher, Hermann, *German Air Force versus Russia*, Arno Press, 1968

Ruge, Friedrich, *Soviets as Naval Opponents*, US Naval Institute Press, 1979

Schueler, Klaus, *Logistik im Russlandfeldzug*, Peter Lang, 1987

Seaton, Albert, *Battle for Moscow*, Stein & Day, 1971

Sharp, Charles, *Soviet Order of Battle in World War Two*, Nafziger, 1996

Spahr, William, *Stalin's Lieutenants*, Presidio, 1997

Stoves, Rolf, *1. Panzer Division, 1939–45*, Hans-Henning Podzun, 1961

Tarleton, Robert, "What Really Happened to the Stalin Line?" parts 1&2, *Journal of Slavic Military Studies*, June 1992 and March 1993

Ueberschar, Gerd, ed., *Unternehmen Barbarossa*, Schoeningh, 1984

Weinberg, Gerhard, *World at Arms*, Cambridge University Press, 1994

Willmott, H.P., *The Great Crusade*, Free Press, 1989

Winters, Harold, *Battling the Elements*, Johns Hopkins University Press, 1998

Wuorinen, John, ed., *Finland and World War Two*, Greenwood, 1983

Zaloga, Stephen, and Leland Ness, *Red Army Handbook, 1939–45*, Sutton Publishing, 1998

Zhukov, Georgi, "The War Begins: The Battle of Moscow" in *Main Front*, Brassey's, 1987

Ziemke, Earl, and Magda Bauer, *Moscow to Stalingrad*, Military Heritage Press, 1988

Ziemke, Earl, and Magda Bauer, *German Northern Theater of Operations, 1940–45*, US Army, 1959

# INDEX

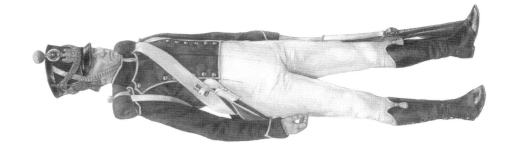

# OSPREY
PUBLISHING

# FIND OUT MORE ABOUT OSPREY

❏ Please send me the latest listing of Osprey's publications

❏ I would like to subscribe to Osprey's e-mail newsletter

Title / rank

Name

Address

City / county

Postcode / zip                    state / country

e-mail

CAM

I am interested in:

❏ Ancient world
❏ Medieval world
❏ 16th century
❏ 17th century
❏ 18th century
❏ Napoleonic
❏ 19th century

❏ American Civil War
❏ World War 1
❏ World War 2
❏ Modern warfare
❏ Military aviation
❏ Naval warfare

Please send to:

**North America**:
Osprey Direct , 2427 Bond Street, University Park, IL 60466, USA

**UK, Europe and rest of world**:
Osprey Direct UK, P.O. Box 140, Wellingborough, Northants, NN8 2FA, United Kingdom

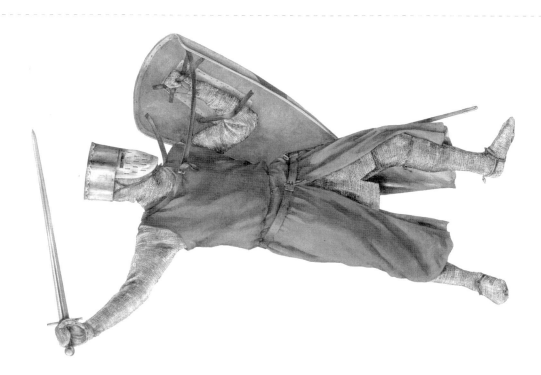

# OSPREY
PUBLISHING

www.ospreypublishing.com

call our telephone hotline
for a free information pack

USA & Canada: 1-800-826-6600
UK, Europe and rest of world call:
+44 (0) 1933 443 863

**Young Guardsman**
Figure taken from *Warrior 22:
Imperial Guardsman 1799–1815*
Published by Osprey
Illustrated by Richard Hook

**Knight, c.1190**
Figure taken from *Warrior 1: Norman Knight 950 – 1204 AD*
Published by Osprey
Illustrated by Christa Hook

POSTCARD